Digital Fortunes

Advance praise for *Digital Fortunes*

'This book offers a seamless blend of storytelling and analytical prowess, making it an effortless page-turner for readers of all backgrounds. It delves into the hidden depths of what truly makes up the digital economy and the scope of its value addition. It is highly informative and without fluff. It contains information pertinent to both value creators and value seekers. Furthermore, the book arrives at the perfect moment as interest in investment and entrepreneurship burgeons across India today. But its relevance extends beyond individual pursuits; policymakers, too, will find wisdom within its pages.'

V. Anantha Nageswaran, Chief Economic Advisor to the Government of India

Digital Fortunes

A Value Investor's Guide to the New Economy

Smarak Swain

BLOOMSBURY
NEW DELHI • LONDON • OXFORD • NEW YORK • SYDNEY

BLOOMSBURY INDIA
Bloomsbury Publishing India Pvt. Ltd
Second Floor, LSC Building No. 4, DDA Complex, Pocket C – 6 & 7,
Vasant Kunj, New Delhi 110070

BLOOMSBURY, BLOOMSBURY INDIA and the Diana logo
are trademarks of Bloomsbury Publishing Plc

First published in India 2024
This edition published 2024

ISBN: PB: 978-93-54354-04-5; e-ISBN: 978-93-54357-13-8
2 4 6 8 10 9 7 5 3 1

Typeset in Fournier MT Std by Manipal Technologies Limited
Printed and bound in India by Thomson Press India Ltd

MIX
Paper | Supporting responsible forestry
FSC® C010615
www.fsc.org

To

02KGP####

The undergrads at IIT Kharagpur who joined in 2002,
and are treading widely different paths

Contents

Preface

The Nobel Prize in Economics for 1997 went to Robert Merton, professor at Harvard University, and Myron Scholes, professor at Stanford University, for developing a pioneering formula for the valuation of stock options. Since the Nobel is no small prize, one would expect the two professors to understand how stock options should be valued. They were also partners in a hedge fund called the Long Term Capital Management (LTCM) which invested in stock options. LTCM almost went bankrupt in 1998 following the Russian financial crisis. It was a huge fund and its bankruptcy could have destabilised the US financial markets, so the US Central Bank intervened and coerced many creditor banks to inject money into LTCM to save it. Having two Nobel laureates, that too ones who received a Nobel Prize for the valuation of stock options, could not save LTCM from doom.

Scholes moved on and set up another hedge fund in 1999 called the Platinum Grove Asset Management (PGAM). Investors in PGAM probably imagined that no one could understand the valuation of stock options better than someone who had developed the best pricing model for them. Unfortunately, PGAM also went bust in November 2008. At that time, Merton was a partner in a hedge fund called the Trinsum Group. This group also went bankrupt two months later.

Commenting on these events, economist Ha-Joon Chang concluded that 'Merton and Scholes did not know what they were doing'.[1] What is true for these Nobel laureates is true for most of us. Neither the economists who make deterministic statements about the economy nor the investment bankers who seem to know the pulse of the market fully understand what they say. Rich people (those who have not inherited their wealth) have earned most of their wealth not by leveraging their skills or entrepreneurial abilities, but by chance. The world today is too complex and the variables are too interconnected to comprehend. Thus, the wise are those who understand the boundaries of their understanding.

It is not easy to come across wise people, or to recognise them as such when we come across them. News channels, the internet, social media – all bombard us with views of influencers, gurus and, worse, experts. To be clear, experts are not trying to con us; most experts have strong convictions, but the convictions are not necessarily correct. In subjects with few random variables, such as constitutional law or rocket science, an expert may still be precise. But this is not so in the case of subjects like political economy, community behaviour and markets. In this precarious landscape of imprecise insights, we often fall for expert advice that confirms our biases or gives us hope to achieve our objectives. Probably the only way to gain reasonable success is to understand the basics of complex phenomena rather than blindly follow the experts.

We are already living in times of rapid transformations due to information and communication technology (ICT). We see changes taking place around us that are multidimensional and all pervasive. The disruptions are going to accelerate even further in this decade, with expected developments in artificial intelligence, 5G technology, the internet of things and cloud-driven applications. The disruptions will affect people, communities, societies, businesses and polities – and we are still grappling to develop a full understanding of ICT's impact.

The landscape of ICT is vast and much beyond the scope of this little book. This book focuses on two sectors of ICT (digital platforms and blockchain technology) and three thematic areas (strengths, vulnerabilities and valuations). Platforms and blockchains are at the centre of a gold rush among investors, both large and small, to get a piece of the wealth expected to be created by firms harnessing these innovations. While there is a frenzy among investors, an understanding of these technologies, the changes they are bringing and the value they are creating is not proportionate to the brouhaha. This book seeks to develop a nuanced understanding of platforms and blockchain-based virtual assets.

One of the areas this book covers is valuation. Now, here is the problem. As stated earlier, Nobel laureates Merton and Scholes tried their hand at the valuation of a class of assets, for which they won the Nobel, but were proved wrong twice in the real world. As a tax officer, I have analysed discounted cash flows (DCF) during tax audits to value companies. My conclusion from years of working in this area is that quantitative methods like DCF are enticing but ignore many extraneous factors that affect a company's valuation. In an article published online, I have demonstrated with a simulation how a small change in just two variables in the Capital Asset Pricing Model leads to a 43 per cent change in enterprise value.[2] In this book I have desisted from making any quantitative valuation. I have also resisted the impulse of simplifying valuation as a multiple of sales (10X valuation is low for a sector,[3] 100X is high for another sector, etc.) or as a derivative of other quantitative factors like customer acquisition cost, customer retention rate and so on.

In this book, I have played more of a role of a tech communicator than an investment adviser (this may have been obvious when I railed against gurus and experts earlier on). My father, Mayadhar Swain, who received the National Award for Outstanding Efforts in Science & Technology Communication through Print Media in 2022, says that the role of a science communicator is to assist readers in comprehension and not to lead the reader towards conclusions. I have learnt a lot from him over the years and have sought to follow his style in writing this book.

I have understood digital technologies from an uncommon vantage point – that of policymakers developing regulations. I have learnt a lot in my interactions with policymakers who are actively developing national laws to cope with the challenges of digitalisation, instituting mechanisms for supervision of the digital economy and negotiating international standards for taxation and regulation in relation to digitalisation. My gratitude to all of them, especially to Rashmi Ranjan Das, Vivek Aggarwal, Ritvik Pandey and Balasubramanian Krishnamurthy of the Department of Revenue, for exposing me to the regulatory challenges arising from digitalisation; to S.S.K. Pradhan and Siddharth Prakash of RBI; Sharad Sharma of SEBI; Amresh Mishra and Jaya Roy of NIA; Amit Kumar and Abhinav Khare of CBI; Shailesh Thakur of FIU-IND; Shashank Misra who handled the Economic Security Cell in the Department of Revenue; Manisha Sinha, Parveen Kumar and Simrandeep Singh from the Department of Economic Affairs; and Deepak Virmani from I4C, for debates and discussions that helped me develop a holistic understanding of cryptocurrencies. Discussions with my wife, Ashima, who is, incidentally, the regulator for the virtual assets sector in FIU-IND, were insightful. I also learnt a lot from the country delegates at the OECD and FATF.

My understanding of digital technologies and how they work developed further during my interactions with batch mates from IIT Kharagpur. Staying true to the IIT Kharagpur tradition, after graduation, my batch mates branched out in many directions and have proved their worth in numerous fields. Those who remained in tech have seen the frontiers of technological progress firsthand and have ridden the waves of the adoption of digital solutions. My understanding of network effects, for both platforms and cryptocurrencies, strongly borrows from their personal and work experiences.

The present form of this book is quite different from the manuscript I first submitted to Bloomsbury India. The editorial efforts of Praveen Tiwari and Nitin Valecha have led to the creation of this book in its present state. I am ever grateful to them for this.

Last but not the least, I am grateful to my mother and my daughter, Dhriti (who was still in preschool when this book was written), for helping me immensely through their encouragement and support throughout the painful writing phase.

The views expressed in this book are purely mine and do not reflect, in any way, the views of the Government of India. I have taken care to ensure that the facts described in the book are picked from public sources, with appropriate reference to such sources. No detail in this book is taken from the official records of the Government of India or any official communication of the government.

Readers should note that investments are subject to market risk, and nothing in this book should be construed as an advisory for making investment decisions.

1

Introduction

This book is not about a stock guru sharing his wisdom, as is usually the case with the 'how-to' books on investing. I do not have the usual qualifications to impart the how-to gyan on investing – neither am I a Warren Buffet or a Rakesh Jhunjhunwala of the stock market, nor have I lost a lot of money and learnt from my mistakes. I have written this book because I see a widespread misunderstanding among investors about the digital economy and how new-age tech companies operate, and how these companies gain and lose value.

New-age tech companies operate in emerging or cutting-edge technology sectors and leverage innovative technologies and business models, often associated with the digital economy, to drive their growth. Traditional methods of valuation do not usually reflect the real value of these companies and so retail investors have nothing much to rely on except market trends. Many investors have lost money and many more will lose money if they don't understand some basics about the valuation of new-age tech companies and how they generate and lose value.

This book was triggered by three events and the response of the investors to them. The first event was the initial public offering (IPO) of Zomato, just a couple of months after the second wave of the COVID-19 pandemic subsided. Zomato is a food delivery company, whose app you might have used to order home delivery from your favourite restaurant. It also manages gig workers who do home delivery of food. The company's IPO valued the company at ₹64,365 crore (a multiple of about 26X of its sales) and was oversubscribed by more than 38 times. Interestingly, retail subscribers, with a quota of 10 per cent, oversubscribed the IPO by 7 times, while the oversubscription by large and institutional investors was 51 times. At that time, the company had been consistently making losses and was yet to make any profit. Only 62 per cent of the shares reserved for employees of Zomato were subscribed. The IPO offered shares of face value ₹1 in a price band between ₹72 and ₹76, the stock's listing price was ₹130.

Started in 2008, Zomato made a loss of ₹1010.51 crore on a revenue of ₹1397.71 crore in financial year (FY) 2018–19. The losses increased to ₹2742.74 crore in FY 2019–20 on revenues of ₹2742.73 crore. In FY 2020–21 (the first pandemic year), its revenue reduced to ₹2118.42 crore and its losses reduced to ₹816.42 crore.[1]

Traditionally, investors value a stock based on the price-to-earning (P/E) ratio. But since this company had no earnings, its price-to-sales ratio was taken by many analysts to assess its valuation. But is it so simple to determine the value of a firm? What if a firm is burning money just to increase sales?

Losses should not be a big worry as long as a company is expected to earn profits in the future. Will Zomato earn enough profits in the future to justify its valuation? To answer this question, we need to understand the platform business model and how business models in the digital economy are different from business models in the traditional economy. As we shall see in the subsequent chapters, there are only two fates of a company following a viable platform model of business – prosper and become a digital giant (or be acquired by one), or collapse and perish. There is no middle ground.

Zomato's Red Herring Prospectus[2] (a full disclosure report submitted by a company to the public after approval from the Securities and Exchange Board of India – SEBI – before floating an IPO) mentioned that it faced intense competition from Swiggy, restaurant chains such as Pizza Hut, McDonald's and Dominos, which have in-house food ordering platforms, and cloud kitchens such as Rebel Foods. It also faced competition from mobile payment applications that facilitate food ordering. Another disclosure in the prospectus was that there were low barriers to entry in the restaurant aggregation industry and the cost of switching between offerings was low. These two disclosures should have been red-flagged by the optimistic investors when considering this stock – for reasons you will know when I explain platform economics. But the retail investors I interviewed were unaware of these two critical issues. These investors contributed to oversubscription of the IPO. Apparently, their reason for investing in Zomato stock was that they used the Zomato app and found it good.

Kunal Bahl, co-founder of e-commerce company Snapdeal, tweeted rather exaggeratedly on the IPO, 'The line between customers and investors gets blurred starting today', to which one of the responses was a light-hearted rejoinder, 'Customers who will now be shareholders will keep ordering to keep their company afloat.'[3]

The people I interviewed had subscribed to Zomato shares with an intent of staying invested for a long period. They were not like the speculators who ride on a wave and plan to exit before the splash. I hoped Zomato succeeded, for their sake. I reprove of what Amitabh Kant, the then CEO of the government think tank Niti Aayog, said in response to the success of the Zomato IPO. In an interview on the TV channel NDTV, the host asked him if the valuation of Zomato on the eve of its offering was 'bit of a bubble'. He replied that for tech start-ups, the acquisition of customers was of paramount importance and drove their value. He gave the example of Amazon to justify the link between the number of customers and valuation that he was arguing about.[4] This statement came from an incomplete understanding of network effects and how they drove value in the digital economy. Such simplistic statements – made by many, not just Kant – mislead people into thinking that the number of customers drives valuation.

If Kant was at one side of the oversimplification spectrum, Harsh Goenka of the industrial conglomerate RPG Group was on the other side. He took a dig at investor response to Zomato's IPO by saying he would also start a foodtech app and incur losses by giving discounts over and above the restaurants' prices and get a successful listing (Figure 1.1).

Zomato is much more than just a cash-burning machine. It is a leading foodtech company with operational bases in twenty-four countries. It hires and manages thousands of gig workers (the food delivery agents) and ensures efficiency in pick-up and delivery of products. It has successful partnerships with restaurants in most urban neighbourhoods of India. The company has valuable business know-how which it has developed through knowing-by-doing. So there is no doubt about Zomato being a valuable company performing a useful role in the market. The question is, how valuable is the company?

Figure 1.1: The other side

Harsh Goenka
@hvgoenka

My newest corporate venture:
I am starting a Swiggy/Zomato like app. I will provide food at 40% discount with a loss of only Rs 3000 cr. If you think the loss is less, I will give 60% discount. I will then list it at Rs 1 lakh cr.
Looking for suckers to invest!

8:03 PM · Jul 17, 2021

10.7K 1.2K Copy link to Tweet

At a fundamental level, shareholders get returns on their capital in the form of a dividend. A company pays dividend out of profits. A company that has incurred heavy losses for years would have eroded its capital base and most likely would have negative reserves (that is, it would have accumulated losses instead of profits). The primary challenge for it will be to make enough profits in the future to make up for past losses and generate a surplus so as to give a good return on the invested capital. Theoretically, the company has an infinite number of years to do this – it is a going concern and there is no deadline. But profit is the only validation of a business model and shareholders will not wait indefinitely for it. Hence, a loss-making company has to turn profitable at some point and start making super-profits to recover the losses and give a decent return on invested capital.

That is why it is not prudent for any company to incur losses – it will later need to make bigger profits to make up the losses. Yet investors have come to view losses as normal for new-age tech companies. For more insights on investor behaviour, it is apt to look at historical parallels. Even though the digital economy is very young, some historical parallels do exist. Internet historian Brian McCullough argues that in the United States in 1999, losing money was a mark of success for internet technology companies. In October 1999, 'the market cap of the 199 internet stocks tracked by Morgan Stanley's Mary Meeker was a whopping US$450 billion. But the total annual sales of these companies came to only about US$21 billion,' he says.[5] Their collective losses totalled US$6.2 billion. The so-called dotcom bubble then burst in 2000 and many of these tech companies lost as much as 80 per cent of their value by the end of 2001. Many of these companies did not recover from their loss in value. Some recovered and went on to become the largest and most powerful tech companies we have today.[6]

The dotcom bubble can be understood by looking at the case of two companies – Pets.com and Amazon. Pets.com started operations in November 1998 and was liquidated in November 2000. A superstar start-up of the pre-dotcom era, it allowed pet owners to buy pet supplies online – it was like an Amazon for pets. It launched a massive marketing campaign, which helped in a dramatic rise of sales. However, the rise in sales was not commensurate with the marketing spend. Between February 1999 and September 1999, the company spent US$11.8 million on advertising, while it generated revenues of just US$619,000. It incurred high shipping costs and lost money on almost every sale.[7] It finally collapsed in November 2000, after raising US$82.50 million in an IPO on the NASDAQ stock exchange in February 2000.

Amazon was an early-stage investor in Pets.com. Although following a similar business model, Amazon could not realise at that time that Pets.com's business was not sustainable. Pet supplies were low-margin, high-volume goods, widely available in grocery stores. The cost of home delivery of heavy pet food packs ate into the narrow margins of the company, thus leading to losses.

Amazon was also severely affected when the dotcom bubble burst and its stock price fell from US$107 to US$7. However, it had a sound business model based on cost optimisation and hence survived the crash.[8] Amazon focussed on selling cheap, but its low sale price was due to operational efficiencies rather than deep discounts. Amazon, which started in 1995 as an online bookseller, also spent significantly on brand building and network reach. Due to all this, it could turn in profits quickly – in the last quarter of 2001 itself. Today it owns key infrastructure in the digital world and ranks among the top ten companies in the world by market capitalisation.

In short, there is good money to be made in the digital economy, but the investor should know where *not* to invest. This is definitely a challenge because of the incomplete understanding about how the digital economy works.

The second trigger for this book is an entrepreneur friend who spent upwards of an year developing a mobile application that brings together Facebook, WhatsApp and Tinder under a single app. The app has three tabs, one for personal messaging, one for private networking and one for social networking. The personal messaging app has a much better user interface than WhatsApp, Telegram or Signal. It promises to protect user privacy by routinely deleting peer-to-peer conversations from its cloud server. It also has some features absent in WhatsApp and Telegram. The private networking tab lets the users choose from random people in their neighbourhood to meet up. Although it allows users to meet strangers sharing common interests, its primary utility is to arrange blind dates. The social networking tab is a rip-off of Facebook, but with better look-and-feel. My friend has been trying for quite some time to raise capital to launch this product. As of now, he is bootstrapping, using his savings from past employment and contributions from relatives. He strongly believes in his idea because his product is much superior to Facebook, WhatsApp, Tinder and a plethora of other apps. A chartered accountant in his network has helped him prepare a valuation report. So he has the product, he has a valuation report and the next logical step seems to be to on-board an angel investor. Unfortunately, merely having a good product does not give you a fighting chance in the digital economy.

Consider this. There has been no start-up with a new search engine since 2008.[9] Google's share in the global search engine market as of November 2023 was 91.54 per cent (Figure 1.2). Its largest competitor was Bing, with a market share of 3.2 per cent.[10]

Google was a late entrant in the search engine business. It built upon several existing ideas and technologies in 1996 and launched its search engine towards the end of 1997.[11] Dominant search engines of the time used keyword-based methods to rank search results. In 1996, Robin Lee developed an algorithm that ranked web pages on the basis of the number of other pages linking to them and patented it. Larry Page, the co-founder of Google, developed a similar algorithm called PageRank in 1998 and patented it. In 2000, Google developed an advertising solution called Adwords as a monetisation strategy. In 2002, Adwords started using a pay-per-click model. The algorithm behind this model was remarkably similar to an algorithm already patented by Overture Services. Overture slapped Google with a lawsuit in late 2002. In 2003, the former was acquired by Yahoo for US$1.63 billion. Google settled the lawsuit in 2004 by giving 2.7 million shares to Yahoo as compensation.[12]

Figure 1.2: Market shares of search engines (June 2009 to November 2023)

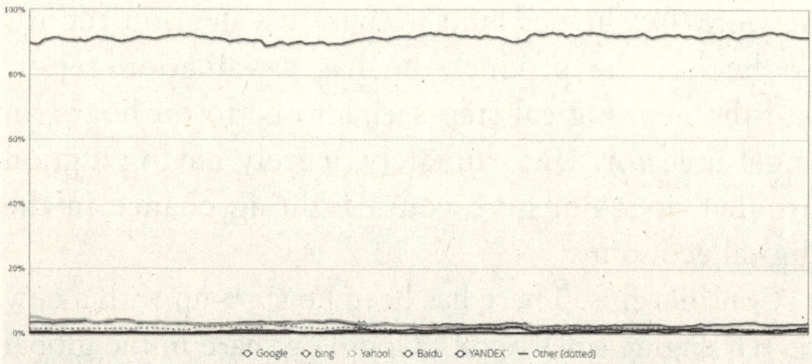

Source: Statcounter

It is clear from Google's rise that only having a good product does not guarantee success in the digital economy. Imitators and adapters have as much of a chance of making it big as an early entrant. Besides, the winner takes all in the digital economy and competition perishes, the luckier ones merging with the winner. The digital economy breeds natural monopolies and we will discuss the reasons for this phenomenon in Chapter 2.

Making incremental changes to an existing product does not help to beat it, especially if the existing product is as entrenched as Facebook or WhatsApp. The entry barriers are just too high to jump across. To trump an incumbent, you need to disrupt its business by coming out with a new solution or a new creative way of delivering the same service.

Entrepreneurs like my friend are important contributors to the economy and society at large. By innovating and building something new, they are moving society ahead on the path of higher prosperity, greater productivity and better quality of life. Mobile apps have changed our lives in ways that we did not even imagine a decade ago. But a sad fact is that for every successful app, there have been a huge number of failed apps in the same segment. Many applications providing us great service today are going to either perish or merge with their competitors. Those that perish will remain unsung and investors won't know anything about them.

When retail investors assess a tech company's stock, they try to make both subjective and objective assessments. When assessing subjectively, they compare the company with the likes of Google, Amazon and Apple – global behemoths who are reaping super-profits because of their monopoly status and market power. However, for every Amazon, there are myriad other companies that perished. But their names do not have the recall value that Amazon has. This biases us in our subjective assessment to view a tech stock more positively than it deserves. While Amazon and Flipkart have become household names in India, the market share of two other e-commerce companies – Snapdeal and ShopClues – have fallen significantly. Many others could not bear the cost of deep discounts typical of this industry and perished.[13]

Objective assessments painstakingly extrapolate the company's performance into the future and predict future profits. Then the future profits are discounted to current times and summed up to value the company. Professional investors rely more on these assessments, but they are equally unreliable. For one, the extrapolation relies on some broad assumptions about the company's growth. Second, it does not consider several extraneous factors that affect the company's future performance. Third, minor changes in assumptions lead to wide changes in the value of the company.

The third trigger for me to write this book was a recent query by my aunt who wanted to invest in a cryptocurrency's initial coin offering (ICO). Much like IPOs, new cryptocurrencies are floated in the market through ICOs. But ICOs are not regulated the way IPOs are regulated. In fact, cryptocurrencies operate in a regulatory vacuum when this book went to print (in early 2023, the Financial Intelligence Unit India – FIU-India – was charged with anti-money-laundering regulation of virtual asset service providers. However, its mandate was limited to ensuring financial integrity and there is still no sector regulator for virtual assets).

Cryptocurrencies are virtual assets that are touted to be substitutes of sovereign-backed currencies. The key conceptual difference is that they are not backed by any sovereign guarantee. The key operational difference is that transactions are verified and recorded through a decentralised system using blockchains and cryptography. Cryptocurrencies are virtual assets. They have no underlying value and their utility is limited. Some of the popular cryptocurrencies such as Bitcoin and Ethereum have become universally accepted by internet users as assets of value, but the less popular ones are purely speculative instruments.

As if the volatility and speculative nature of these virtual assets was not enough, they have faced consistent regulatory action around the world. The regulatory onslaught on cryptocurrencies in India started in late 2017 with an all-India income tax survey on cryptocurrency exchanges. The purpose of the survey was purportedly to collect information on cryptocurrency traders and investors on these exchanges and verify if they were paying taxes on their gains from trading in cryptos.[14] In April 2018, the Reserve Bank of India (RBI) issued a circular directing banks not to provide banking services to customers for dealing in cryptocurrencies. The 2018 action of the RBI placed a de facto ban in India on cryptocurrencies. This circular was set aside by the Supreme Court in March 2021. However, cryptocurrency transactions still face significant risk of taxes and penalty under the Income Tax Act and Goods and Services Tax (GST) Act. India's annual budget of 2022 introduced a new regime to tax gains from transactions in virtual digital assets. While this new regime presents many challenges to investors in cryptocurrencies, it does not clarify whether cryptocurrency trading is legal in India.[15]

Crypto-trading is gradually gaining legitimacy with several developments in 2023 and early 2024. In March 2023, virtual digital assets (a wider asset class that includes cryptocurrencies) were brought under the ambit of the Prevention of Money Laundering Act, 2002. Exchanges and brokers dealing in virtual digital assets were required to comply with certain anti-money-laundering regulations and report suspicious transactions to FIU-India. As of end-2023, thirty-one exchanges and brokers had registered with FIU-India. On 29 December 2023, FIU-India declared that it was taking action against nine offshore exchanges that were located remotely and operated in the Indian market but did not register with FIU-India. Through a press release,

FIU-India branded the exchanges not registered with it as 'operating illegally', implying that those registered with it were operating legally. This still does not impart a full legitimacy to crypto assets. Since there is no sector regulator, there is no one to tell the exchanges which crypto assets to deal in. Any cross-border transaction in crypto assets runs the risk of violating multiple rules under the Foreign Exchange Management Act (FEMA). A few other issues will be discussed in Chapter 5.

The nature of the asset, the volatility, the regulatory risks and the uncertainty make cryptocurrency one of the worst asset classes to make rational investment in. And yet, investors have a fear of missing out (FOMO) and many invest in crypto assets without an inkling about what it is.

I had highlighted the persistent presence of Ponzi schemes in my book *The Great Indian Fraud*. Such schemes keep recurring because retail investors do not actually understand much about finance. The story of crypto investors is similar. In a survey conducted in 2021 among crypto investors in the United Kingdom, it was found that 36 per cent had 'poor or non-existent' knowledge of the sector when they first invested in cryptocurrencies. Also, 21 per cent of investors admitted that they still knew nothing about cryptocurrencies.[16] No wonder, ICOs have become a favourite source for Ponzi schemers to raise money from the public.

Some early investors have made handsome money from Bitcoin, Ethereum and other cryptocurrencies. Many speculators have managed to move with the volatile swings in the price of popular cryptocurrencies and have made tidy profits. Some of them have become evangelist advocates of cryptos. When I ask these advocates about a cryptocurrency's underlying value, they ask me about the intrinsic value of rupee-denominated notes and gold. If someday a cryptocurrency becomes accepted currency for international transactions, it would definitely rise to the level of US Dollar or Japanese Yen or the Euro – anchor currencies that have no intrinsic value but are stores of value nevertheless. Bitcoin has near anchor-currency status in the international underground market of drug traffickers, child-pornography producers, hitmen, mujahideen and whatnot. This book will delve into cryptos and related concepts like non-fungible tokens (NFTs), decentralised finance (DeFi) and stablecoins and discuss which of them are rational investments.

Most are not. Not every cryptocurrency gains the status and utility of Bitcoin. The website coinmarketcap.com lists 8,962 different cryptocurrencies.[17] Some of these are fronts for Ponzi and pyramid schemes and money-laundering rackets. Investing in just any cryptocurrency is unwise, unless the investor has insider information about a large investor hoarding the crypto for doomsday, or some similar event. Investing in the ICO of a cryptocurrency that is not yet in the market is foolish. But still, there is a consistent demand for ICOs. Ample people are eager to invest their hard-earned money in cryptos, but without the patience to understand what cryptos are.

Coming back to my aunt, I managed to convince her not to put her money in the particular ICO. She then put the money she had earmarked for cryptos into a private scheme, peddled by a neighbour, that promised her an interest of 10 per cent per month. I saved my aunt from the frying pan, but who can save an investor bent upon jumping into the fire?

You may wonder what qualifications I have to pass judgements on stocks and assets operating in the digital economy, as I have made scant investments on the stock market, due to certain job constraints. As a career taxman, I have been privy to certain insider information that could affect my investment decisions. I have conducted tax audits of more than a thousand companies from diverse backgrounds. I have audited pricing and valuation strategies used in merger and acquisition (M&A) activities by some of the largest multinational enterprises operating in India. I have also conducted financial investigations on various corporate groups. In a recent diplomatic role, I have been a part of India's delegation in the Organisation for Economic Co-operation and Development (OECD) to solve the tax challenges arising out of digitalisation of the economy. My knowledge of financial data and details not available publicly could unduly influence my choice of stocks to invest in. Hence, I consider active investing in the stock market to be against my professional ethics.

Nevertheless, I may be just qualified enough to explain the business models that click in the digital world. My idea here is to introduce you to the digital economy – how it works, why it does not work the way traditional economy works, and a framework that can be used to analyse assets related to the digital economy. While making investment decisions, it is equally important to know where not to invest. This book aspires to help you bridge the gap between *risk* and *uncertainty*. Risk is quantifiable, while uncertainty is not. When you face the prospect of investing in a start-up that makes recurring losses but makes tall claims, you are judging an uncertain future. But if you know the value-drivers in the digital economy, you can evaluate the risks involved and take an informed decision.

Two-sided platforms, social networks, virtual assets and other such innovations in the digital economy open up myriad opportunities to solve problems and remove constraints. The companies which manage to successfully use these tools to provide solutions become enduring technology brands. In Chapter 2, we will see how the digital economy is different from traditional economies and how successful companies in the digital space have made their profits. Chapter 3 will investigate the growth of tech giants and the disproportionate growth in their power and influence. Chapter 4 will delve into the vulnerabilities that platform businesses face. Chapter 5 will introduce virtual assets, classify them into types (to make sense of the plethora of cryptocurrencies in vogue) and conduct a risk assessment of different virtual asset classes. Chapter 6 will highlight the shortcomings in the promise of cryptocurrencies, ending in an analysis of the cryptocurrencies that will survive the test of time.

The internet has drastically changed our ways of living and connecting with one another. It has increased productivity manifold and has changed the workplace at a fundamental level. Many people have become rich by making the right investment in internet technologies. Many more will become rich. A second, once-in-a-lifetime opportunity is coming within a single lifetime, in the form of the Fourth Industrial Revolution. The Fourth Industrial Revolution builds on the digital revolution by introducing new technologies to intricately connect the physical world with the digital world. There is much money to be made by investing in new-age tech companies which will own a piece of the digital world after the Fourth Industrial Revolution. But making the right investment will require deep insights and perspectives. I hope to provide some of them in this book.

2

Platform Economics

MindGeek is one of the largest tech companies in the world. More than 115 million users visit its websites daily, almost as much as YouTube.[1] Every day, users upload about 15 terabytes of data on its websites, which is roughly half of Netflix's total content.[2] The company proudly describes itself as a 'global industry-leading information technology firm' on its website. Yet, there is a good chance that you have never heard of this company.

MindGeek is one of the new-age tech companies which have tasted instant success by harnessing the power of platforms. To fully comprehend what Mindgeek does, we need to go back a little in time. In the 1990s, there were a large number of dingy, single screen theatres featuring the so-called adult or blue films. The shady movies airing in these theatres were the subject of intense conversations among college students. Some adventurous types would dare to go and watch these films. These folks would have an air of superiority around them during class breaks. A few others would not boast but would quietly don monkey caps to hide their identity and sneak into the theatres to watch the films. By all accounts, these theatres were dirty and unhygienic.

Then came the porn video cassettes and DVDs in the late 1990s. A person could easily purchase them from stores and watch them in the privacy of their bedrooms. But there was a cost attached to that. Some deviant entrepreneurs in colleges would rent them out to classmates. In IIT Kharagpur, depraved students staying in campus hostels would share the expenses and watch pondy in hostel common rooms ('pondy' is an IIT lingo, meaning Pornographic Details for the Youth, and refers to porn videos). The story is the same in many residential colleges. Alumni who were in hostels in those times insist that watching pondy together created brotherly bonds, which were absent among students after the internet became widely accessible.

Exactly what changed when the internet became widely accessible? Well, porn clips became available free-of-cost on porn channels. This has been a transformative change from the time when consumers had to manage multiple gatekeepers to procure and watch blue films. Both demand and supply scenario in this industry have changed dramatically. Consumption of pornographic material has increased exponentially ('demand increase' does sound like a bad thing when using the porn industry for illustration). In 2018, the website Pornhub had 33.5 billion visits[3] (the world population at the time was 7.53 billion), with 63,992 new visitors every minute, watching 207,405 videos through 57,750 searches.[4] India ranked third in the number of viewers by country.

On the supply side, porn theatres perished and the entire supply chain of blue films was disrupted. The industry saw widespread diversification in content, with performers specialising in different fetishes – BDSM, podophilia, cosplay, MILF fetish, inter-racial and whatnot. Performers could now build their individual brand on the Pornhub platform and were not dependent on a long supply chain consisting of producers, distributors, theatres and DVD shops, to reach the customer. The Pornhub Model Programme contained over 10,000 independent performers who received a share of advertisement revenues generated from their uploads.

This revolution (in less than two decades) is not limited to the porn industry. Digital technology has transformed every sector, every industry and every market. This transformation is a new way of doing business called the 'platform model'. The purpose of taking the porn industry as an example is to demonstrate how this revolution has affected even a heavily censored and regulated industry as porn.

The agent of transformation in the porn industry was MindGeek, which owns Pornhub as well as YouPorn, GayTube, Digital playground and Brazzers. MindGeek was inspired by another platform, YouTube, which started in 2005. YouTube allowed users to upload video content for other users to watch. By providing free infrastructure (which included the website, the user interface, the storage and facilities to 'like' and comment on the videos), YouTube became a significant platform for users to interact and share videos. Pornhub and Xvideos soon took the same model and replicated it for their business. They run web platforms that connect content producers and performers with porn viewers. Porn viewers get an ever-increasing array of videos to choose from, all at no cost. Content producers and performers get a share of ad revenues and entice a few of these viewers towards paid services such as live cams and subscription videos. That is, the platform unlocks new sources of value for both producers and consumers.

One reason for Pornhub's success was the fact that users could upload pirated videos on the website without copyright problems. A platform is subject to copyright regulations and has to withdraw pirated content upon request of the copyright owner. However, 'obscene' videos do not get the legal shelter of copyright in many jurisdictions.[5] So there was a huge amount of content available on the website for which no expenses were incurred to produce or acquire.

Platforms generate value for the two sides that connect over them. The platform business model existed before the internet, but the spread of the internet has enabled platform businesses to grow huge in scale and scope. They have the potential to earn super-profits by leveraging their position and power in the digital economy and that is why there is a gold rush to purchase their stocks. But first, it is important to understand how these businesses are different from traditional business.

Pipelines vs Platforms

Traditionally, businesses created value by playing a role that had some importance in a supply chain. The supply chain consisted of manufacturers, traders, distributors and service providers. Value was created in each step of the supply chain. This system was optimised by enhancing quality and lowering cost in each step of the supply chain. Large multinational enterprises (MNEs) of the pre-digital era owed their success to global value chains. They sourced goods and services from the locations where these inputs were available at the lowest cost. They passed on a part of the cost saved to consumers, something that small firms could not do. Further, they optimised the processes in each step to enhance the quality of the goods and services delivered. In this manner, global firms gained a competitive advantage over local firms.

This linear structure is also described as a pipeline.[6] Take the example of toys in a Firstcry showroom in Mumbai. First, Firstcry sets up a subsidiary in China for quality control and sourcing support. This subsidiary places orders with a manufacturer of toys in China and ensures that the manufacturer maintains the requisite quality. The toys are then shipped to a Firstcry warehouse in India, from where the toys are sent to Firstcry stores as well as other toy stores. Firstcry stores are franchisees of Firstcry and make retail sales. The entire process works in a pipeline. Value is created in each stage of the pipeline and flows linearly in one direction – from the producer to the consumer.

Platforms, in contrast, generate value by connecting customers and businesses. An example of a platform in the traditional economy is a stock exchange. Companies, traders and investors approach the stock exchange for different purposes. Companies go to the exchange to list their shares after raising capital through an IPO. Traders approach the stock exchange to trade in stocks. The stock exchange is a platform that provides a service to them – it connects these diverse people, firms and groups of people. It provides a platform through which these different actors can connect. The platform provides important services to all of them. It sets the rules of interactions, maintains control over the interactions, collects relevant data on transactions taking place on the platform and charges a fee on each transaction. A trader may make money one day and lose money another day, but the exchange always makes money.

Although the platform business model existed before the advent of internet, it was not the dominant model for generating value and running a successful business. This was because a platform generates value by building connections, and before the internet, there was a limit to the size of such connections in different businesses. In pre-internet times, connections were physical and time consuming. Internet technology revolutionised the way people connected with one another and has thus enabled platforms to grow bigger and become dominant. Thus, the internet revolution has led to the platform revolution.

We can find both pipeline and platform business models in the digital economy. Digital companies such as Oyo Rooms, Urban Clap (now Urban Company), Swiggy, Bharat Matrimony and Practo are platforms. Pepperfry, Urban Ladder, Unacademy and Pizza Hut (home delivery app) are pipeline businesses. Urban Ladder, for example, sells furniture online. A traditional pipeline business would sell furniture offline, from stores or shops. By going online, Urban Ladder has a wider reach. However, its business model is still the same. It purchases furniture from someone and sells it to someone else. It derives value not from building connections, but by performing its functions efficiently in a supply chain of furniture. In this sense, Urban Ladder is not much different from furniture sellers like Godrej Interio or Damro or Nilkamal. There may be differences in the product range they sell or in the customer segment these companies cater to, but their business model and business segments are the same. Most traditional businesses are going online and the digitalisation process has accelerated due to the COVID-19 pandemic. Incidentally, Godrej Interio, Damro and Nilkamal have dedicated websites through which you can place an order for their furniture from the comfort of home.

Digital Platforms

Platform businesses have few parallels in the traditional economy. Ola does not own any taxi. It connects taxi drivers with riders. Due to the possibilities of internet technology, it could scale up to become one of the largest ride-hailing companies of India. Urban Company offers home installation, maintenance, repair, home exercise and home beauty services. However, it is only a marketplace connecting gig workers with consumers. When I locate a barber through the Urban Company app for a haircut at home, I know that he is not an employee of the company – he is a gig worker. Before this app brought this innovation, I either lined up at a neighbourhood barber shop for a haircut, or I called home a barber I was acquainted with. This app has enabled me to connect with an array of service providers. It has opened new supply channels for both the consumer and the gig worker. The consumer gets ample suppliers of services to choose from, while the worker is presented with new sources of gig work.

Matchmaking platforms like shaadi.com and matrimony.com have revolutionised the ways arranged marriage (a social norm and not a business) happens in India where matchmaking has been a hobby or a social preoccupation during most of history. It is usually the elders in the family who hunt for matches in kin groups. In Jane Austen's *Emma*, the protagonist tries to match men and women in her limited social network of 19th-century England without any profit motive. In India we know of *bichauliyas* or professionals who would act as intermediaries in matchmaking. These persons would take fees from both sides and organise meetings between the prospective bride and groom families. A typical bichauliya would carry photographs of prospective brides and grooms along with the horoscopes and biodata of each candidate. Classified ads in newspapers were another source through which people found leads for marriage proposals.

Nothing like Bharat Matrimony existed before the digital economy came of age. This website is part of the matrimony.com group, which found an opportunity to create value in a social process by providing a platform to prospective brides and grooms to come together. To be clear, there have been several instances of matchmaking platforms in the past. In many local traditions, seasonal fairs provide a facility to young people to meet and court potential spouses. In an extreme case, in one area in Japan in the 7th century, mass orgies were conducted in both spring and autumn in a ritual called *utagaki*. It was one of the best chances of wooing persons of the opposite sex from outside the village. Couples formed during utagaki went on to wed subsequently. Utagaki was a platform that built connections between two sides – men and women looking for partners.

But Bharat Matrimony is a very different kind of platform. It connects men and women throughout the length and breadth of the country, and their anxious parents, through an online application. The platform gives the user facilities for sharing profiles, photographs, horoscopes and other information. It allows a user to chat with a match, or block a mismatch from chatting and much more. A person can search for a prospective spouse of specific height, weight, colour, race, religion, caste group, profession, income group and citizenship (apparently some persons only want spouses with American green cards). Bharat Matrimony provides its services free because this helps the company attract a large number of users. It charges for special services, and these subscriptions constitute 90 per cent of its revenues. It earns the rest from marriage-related services such as sale of matrimonial gifts and return gifts, and publishing matrimony directories.[7]

Some parallels can be drawn between the platforms run by MindGeek and matrimony.com. In both cases, the platforms provide facilities to users, but do not charge them for these facilities because their objective is to build and grow a network of users. This network of users is a business asset that can be monetised in different ways. Monetisation is possible by providing special services for a fee, or by harnessing the data generated by users, or by selling complementary products to them.

Platforms make losses for many years while they build their network of users. This is because in the initial years of operations, the platform has to spend a significant amount of money on acquiring and on-boarding users. For example, in the case of matrimony.com, it started operations in 1997 but broke even and made profits only in 2009.[8] A bachelor looking for a partner would not use its platform if he failed to find sufficient number of female users and vice versa. In the initial years, the company's key challenge was to bring male users on board even if there were not enough female users on the platform and also to bring female users on board even if there were not enough male users.

Digital Pipelines

We will come back to the features of the platform business model later. For now, it is important to place platforms and pipelines in perspective. Platforms are the real deal. These companies have the potential to turn your investment into gold. Due to reasons narrated later, the right platform company has a potential of increasing in value exponentially. This is what you should look for if you are investing in stocks of new-age tech companies. Pipeline companies should be assessed by investors the same way their competitors in the traditional economy are assessed. They might have got a head start in digital penetration, but their competitors would soon catch up. A competitor that does not digitise its business processes at the right time will perish, for digitisation brings numerous efficiency advantages. Every traditional company is digitising. In fact, the entire economy is getting digitalised.

To understand the pipeline business model better, I went on a tour to Rajinder Nagar in New Delhi. This area is one of the three major hubs of coaching for civil service exams, and it is in the middle of a major disruption. I had stayed in Rajinder Nagar for some 6–8 months when I was preparing for the civil service examinations in 2007.

Coaching institutes of numerous specialisations have sprouted in every nook and corner of Rajinder Nagar. The Goliath among them used to be Vajiram & Ravi. It had the best teachers, the maximum number of students and the highest number of successes in successive entrance exams. Of course, if you have high student enrolment, there is a good chance that you will have the lion's share of students in the civil service examination merit list, though the percentage or rate of success may or may not be high.

Nevertheless, there have been many disruptors in this space in the recent years. Unacademy is a prominent name among them. Unacademy is a Bengaluru-based edtech start-up, started in 2015 by a serial entrepreneur and a former Indian Administrative Service (IAS) officer. In September 2020, the company raised US$150 million (about ₹1,100 crore at prevailing exchange rates then) at a valuation of US$1.45 billion and attained the status of a 'unicorn' (in venture capitalist lingo, a unicorn is a company valued at above US$1 billion).

Unacademy provides a plethora of free classes on YouTube as well as on its website. These free classes are recorded videos that anyone can watch. It charges a subscription fee in case a student wants to take live classes for civil service coaching (also for IIT JEE, CAT and many other competitive examinations now). The subscription fee covers live classes, live tests and quizzes, and access to some recorded videos not available free. This business model is typically called 'freemium', that is, give free content hoping that some customers would buy paid content from you.

A freemium model is different from a platform model. While users share free content on platforms like YouTube and Pornhub (and the platform incurs no expense producing them), Unacademy has to make and post its own recorded videos free for students. Upon doing a cursory search on YouTube, I realised that many tutors also work on the freemium model and release some of their videos free for students. Such videos act as advertisements for the paid content of the tutors. Fundamentally, Unacademy's model is a pipeline business model. It has tutors on contract whom it pays for delivering lectures. It packages these lectures and sells them to consumers for a subscription fee. Its key innovation is that it provides lectures through the online medium.

Whether live virtual classes increase or decrease productivity in the teaching process is a still an open question. There are many advantages of virtual classes. They are cheaper, because it is possible to disseminate the same video to an infinite number of students. Students can take the classes in flexitime and do not have to be physically present in a classroom. At the same time, some benefits of the traditional classroom are missing in virtual classes. According to psychologists and sociologists, social interactions, collaboration with peers and meaningful discussions in a classroom are critical to the learning process.[9] They are absent in online classes. Some educators now advocate for hybrid learning that mixes the benefits of both online and offline teaching.

I went for a site-walk of the Rajinder Nagar coaching hub to understand how successful online coaching has been in disrupting physical coaching. This was a couple of months after the second wave of the COVID-19 pandemic had devastated Delhi. I was surprised to find a significant number of aspirants loafing around the Old Rajinder Nagar market. Upon querying, I found that while a majority of the aspirants had returned to their hometowns due to the pandemic, many had stayed back. Most traditional coaching centres were conducting classes online and practice tests were also online. These aspirants had not gone home because staying in Rajinder Nagar helped them in exchanging notes and ideas with peers. Further, they could meet their tutors in person to discuss thorny concepts and get doubts resolved.

Here comes the interesting part. The online coaching most students in this hub seemed to prefer was from Vajiram & Ravi, followed by NextIAS.[10] Both are traditional coaching institutes and were forced to go completely online due to the pandemic. One bookstore owner told me that Vajiram & Ravi had promised to start classroom coaching again as soon as possible, bowing to the heavy demand, but would also continue their online programmes for outstation students. The aspirants I met were ambivalent about online classes. Many appreciated the ease of information dissemination, but expressed problems in maintaining attention for long periods.

One aspirant told me that the internet was flooded with freemium. There was no dearth of study material and video lectures covering the syllabus, although most of the questions asked in the civil service examinations can be answered using content from Wikipedia and newspapers. What serious aspirants needed was clarity of concepts, insights into public policy and assistance in writing answers. He selected the institute that, in his view, best coached in these areas. The medium – online or offline – was not important to him.

I took a walk in Rajinder Nagar again in January 2024 and found that students were back in crowds, implying that the online coaching that had increased during the pandemic did not become a habit.

Unacademy is in competition with entrenched firms in civil service coaching. The same is the scenario in other areas like IIT JEE coaching, medical entrance coaching and CAT coaching, and the organisation has to demonstrate how it is better than the competition.

In a way, Unacademy's business model is similar to that of over-the-top (OTT) channels such as Netflix, Hotstar, Eros Now and AltBalaji. Yet, OTT has been a much bigger force of disruption in the content segment than Unacademy or Byju's have been in the edtech segment. Byju's was the edtech industry leader for years, but was facing an existential crisis in early 2024. Netflix, the pioneer of OTT, came up with the idea of TV-on-demand in 1997, when video streaming on the internet was in its infancy. At that time, entertainment content was supplied through TV channels and followed a schedule determined by the managers of the TV channels. The supply side called all the shots, while the demand side could only consume the broadcasted content. Netflix disrupted this equation with its TV-on-demand offering. In its initial years, the company supplied content through DVDs on rent, and it was only in 2007 that it started providing content through online streaming.[11] Even though OTT and online coaching are both pipelines, OTT is a fundamental innovation in business, while online coaching is not.

Investing in Digital Pipelines

Digital disruption has taken place in two stages. In stage 1, digital pipeline companies disrupted traditional pipeline companies wherever they could digitise distribution to reach a large market at a low cost. In stage 2, platforms disrupted pipelines.

So should you invest in digital pipeline businesses or stay away from them? The answer is, yes, invest in them.

Digital pipeline businesses definitely add value, but should be evaluated against the same metrics used to evaluate traditional pipeline companies. My classmate from IIT Kharagpur has co-founded Stanza Living, a start-up providing hostel accommodation in all major cities of India. Stanza Living, and other start-ups like Zolo stays and Nestaway, promise standardised amenities and services in their hostels. They are pipeline chains of hostels and immediately evoke a comparison with the likes of Young Men's Christian Association (YMCA). However, Stanza Living allows the customer to interact with the management for bookings, check-in and service requests, all through its app. Its app-based services for residents create a high level of standardisation. The data the company collects on residents' preferences and peeves is used to prioritise services and increase efficiency.

An investor should check how a company utilises data while evaluating its stock. Digital pipelines collect significant data on consumer choice, which they could use in production-related decision making. The larger its digital footprint, more is the data a digitalised company can collect and utilise. In the case of Netflix, its Chief Communications Officer disclosed that Netflix uses data from 'user interactions to gauge consumer interest in new programming and to determine how best to categorize and present existing programming.'[12] The success of *The House of Cards* starring Kevin Spacey is often attributed to data analytics. Apparently, Netflix analysed the viewing patterns of the original UK series *The House of Cards* and concluded that the fans of this series would also be interested in content starring Kevin Spacey or directed by David Fincher. This led them to a decision to make a fresh version of the series with David Fincher, starring Kevin Spacey. Netflix was so confident of its success that it committed US$100 million for two seasons, even before the series started.[13]

Insight from consumer data can help a company take the right executive decisions and trump any competitor who does not have such data. In this way, data acts as an entry barrier for competitors and can help the company earn monopoly profits and boost the value of its stock.

The Modus Operandi of Platforms

Platform stocks can provide much more superior returns compared to pipeline stocks. The value in pipeline businesses generally grows in proportion to the growth of business. But the value in platform businesses grows exponentially as the business grows. That is why platform stocks are attractive to invest in.

A platform is a two-sided market, that is, it provides services to two sets of customers. Its economics was discussed in a classic paper of 2002, titled 'Platform Competition in Two-Sided Markets' by Jean-Charles

Rochet and Jean Tirole. The value of the platform for the customers on one side increases with the increase in the number of customers on the other side and vice versa. This can be explained through the example of a dating app.

In a typical dating app, the user browses through profiles of users of the opposite sex and evinces interest on the app. If two users like each other's profile, the app connects them and they can then chat with each other. Men are one group of customers and women are another group of customers. The app is of value to a male user if the number of women using the app is large. The larger the number of profiles of women on the app, the more is the value of the app for men. Similarly, the larger the number of profiles of men to choose from, the more the app's value for women.

The platform faces an important challenge in the beginning stage in managing the two-sided markets. Customers on the first side would not join the platform unless a sufficient number of customers on the second side had already joined. Similarly, customers on the second side would not join unless a sufficient number on the first side had already joined. This is a chicken-and-egg problem that most platforms face. To tackle this, many platforms provide large incentives to users and hence incur heavy losses. For instance, Ola used to offer mind boggling discounts and attractive referral fees to riders. On the other side of the platform, cab drivers were offered very high remuneration to attract them to join. Both riders and drivers were puzzled about how a rider paid less to the platform than what the driver made on the same booking. In short, Ola offered its services at a price below the marginal cost.[14]

It is common for platform businesses to make losses during initial years of operation in any new market. They are basically trying to solve the chicken-and-egg problem by onboarding customers as well as suppliers with heavy incentives and deep discounts. Loss is common for platforms till they build a stable network of customers, but it is difficult for many investors to envision a company that makes losses consistently for years.

These companies can be viewed as traditional companies with long gestation periods. For example, let us consider power plants. Coal-fuelled power plants have a much shorter gestation period than hydropower plants. Coal-fuelled power plants require a low capital investment but have a high revenue expenditure as the input (coal) is costly. Hydropower plants require a high capital investment and have a long gestation period before the investments can be recovered. But their revenue expenditure is minimal and the input (water) is free and renewable.

Platform businesses have a high gestation period during which they earn less than they burn, while they build a network of customers on the two sides of the market. This insight can have very interesting and also some very bizarre consequences. A platform business needs to be extremely disciplined in order to spend but not overspend. The business needs to be clear about its strategy for making profits at some particular time in the future, which is usually not very obvious at a time when their immediate goal is to increase their network at the cost of the bottom line. This attribute of platform companies also means that traditional accounting does not capture the value they create. When platform companies draw up their financial statements using traditional accounting parameters, they end up showing heavy losses and negative net worth; the value they generate is in the network of users they have created, but such intangible assets are often not recorded in financial statements.

Equally befuddled by the accounting results of platform companies as a common investor, some tax officers decided to set the situation right in their own way. They found that the ecommerce marketplace Flipkart sold goods at a price lower than the purchase price in fiscal years 2011–12 to 2014–15. As an example, assume that the total purchase price was ₹100 lakh, the sale price was ₹80 lakh, leading to a loss at gross level of ₹20 lakh (actual amounts were much more; Flipkart India had declared a loss of ₹796 crore in its income tax return for FY 2014–15).[15] It is natural for a business to make losses at the net level, due to inefficiencies and business conditions. Nevertheless, a company usually operates with a profit motive. Consistently selling at a price below cost year-after-year means the primary motive of the company is something else. The tax officers auditing Flipkart India's accounts concluded that the company was following a predatory pricing strategy and the intention of deep discounts was to increase its reach in the Indian market. Having concluded this, the tax officers treated Flipkart's discounts as capital expenditure to develop intangibles and removed the discounts from the revenue account. This effectively converted its losses into taxable income in some of the years audited by the tax officers.

In the appeal proceedings in the tax tribunal, Flipkart India took the plea that the tax department can tax an income that has arisen or accrued, not a hypothetical income. Further, the tax officer cannot compute income in a manner that he desires by completely disregarding the financial records maintained as per accounting standards. The tax tribunal concurred with Flipkart India's arguments and struck down the tax department's order.[16]

Notwithstanding the merits of the tax department's case against Flipkart, the tax officers' action highlights the perplexity they faced with traditional accounting being used for platform businesses. Platform companies burn money to on-board customers on the two sides of the market. This leads to a network of users mediated by the platform, which is their biggest asset. Unfortunately, many retail investors do not clearly understand this. Some investors generalise this propensity to incur losses to all tech companies, irrespective of whether they are platform or pipeline companies. They aggressively invest in persistently loss-making pipeline companies because they feel loss is natural for all tech companies. Many others remain sceptical of platform companies merely because they incur losses.

After the start-up phase, a platform business starts making money by charging a fee for interactions through the platform. The platform need not charge equal amounts from both sides. It can charge one side of the market and provide services to the other side free, or charge more from one side than the other. Rochet and Tirole observe, 'Attracting one side by lowering price is particularly profitable for the platform if this side creates substantial externalities on the other side.'[17] For instance, Flipkart does not charge any commission from buyers; it charges commission only from sellers. Google provides internet search services free to customers and only charges advertisers. Ola includes its service fees in the bill raised on riders but does not charge the drivers.

The pricing policies of platforms are ever evolving, and some emerging social problems, such as pitiable working conditions of gig workers, are being linked to such policies. Gig workers are temporary workers who take up contingent work through online platforms. They enter into contract with the platform and constitute one side of a two-sided platform. The platform connects their demand for work with consumers' demand for services. But in effect, these are workers reporting to an application programming interface (API). Because of a contractual relationship with the platform, they do not receive any pension or health insurance. Platforms face a dual incentive for minimising their wages to the extent possible. First, lower the service cost to consumers, more will be the number of consumers on the platform. Second, the more the number of consumers on the platform, the more will be the opportunity for gig work on the platform and more gig workers will come onboard. With large numbers of workers looking for assignments, gig workers lose all bargaining power in the process and have to settle for low wages. The platform not only connects consumers with gig workers, it also sets the rules, maintains control over the transaction and sets the transaction price. In effect, because the platform tries to serve consumers cheap, it recovers its fees from the other side – gig workers.

For example, there are three different kinds of users on a food delivery platform – restaurants, consumers and delivery boys. This platform is a multi-sided market. The consumer pays a composite amount, which goes towards (a) the food, (b) the delivery charges and (c) the platform's commission. The platform may not charge a commission in the start-up phase and may even give deep discounts over and above the restaurant's sale price. But in the long run, it has to earn a commission in order to sustain the business. Zomato and Swiggy, the two major food delivery platforms in India, charge a commission from restaurateurs and not consumers.

However, in order to retain consumers in the long term, such a platform's delivery also has to be quick and cheap. To retain customers, and make some money in the process, it has to brutally optimise delivery. The platform would require gigs to work within time constraints and take low remuneration. This has not created major labour issues yet, but delivery persons have raised their voice many times against 'exploitation' by food-tech platforms.[18] Sooner or later, labour conditions prevailing in the gig economy will motivate gig workers to organise and demand social security and humane regulations in their contractual terms. Already in the United Kingdom, the Supreme Court has ruled that Uber drivers should be treated as workers and not self-employed entrepreneurs. As per the UK's Supreme Court, the drivers are eligible for minimum wages, private pensions and paid holidays.[19]

Network Effects

As the first wave of COVID-19 pandemic struck, two books on taxation I had written ran out of print. One was a technical analysis of valuation and arms' length pricing of patents, brands and other business intangibles. The other was a book admonishing tax avoidance strategies (pompously titled *Loophole Games: A Treatise on Tax Avoidance Strategies*; it was meant as a sermon against tax avoidance but ended up – much to my chagrin – being used by students of accounts and law as a *how-to* book on tax avoidance). Both titles were published by WoltersKluwer India, a subsidiary of the Dutch publisher WoltersKluwer. WoltersKluwer India had two divisions at the time, medical books and audit books. As the pandemic started, the publisher concluded that its audit books vertical was not viable anymore and decided to return the publishing rights to the authors. And my two tax titles became orphans.

But other traditional publishers of tax books, including some established names, soon approached me with offers to publish these two titles. Apparently, WoltersKluwer's decision was seen as an opportunity by other publishers. The tax portal Taxsutra also approached me with an offer to publish my book. It had just got into the book publishing business and had no experience to back its pitch. Curiously, it had decided not to get into physical book publishing. For print copies, it would onboard a 'print partner' which would be an established traditional publisher. The print partner would engage in editing, binder development, printing and distribution through traditional distribution channels. It appeared that Taxsutra was not really bringing anything to the table, but I finally went ahead with it for reasons I shall mention shortly.

Taxsutra was founded in 2010 by two reporters and a chartered accountant. The start-up obtained rulings of tax tribunals, High Courts and the Supreme Court on tax matters and reported them on its portal. It worked on a subscription model, in which they gave access to the rulings and other tax reports to users who included tax professionals, tax managers in corporations and tax officers, in return for a subscription fee. This was a typical pipeline business model, which was already followed by other tax-news reporting portals in India and elsewhere.

But Taxsutra went a step ahead. It realised that the community of tax professionals was a small one, but widely dispersed. It tried to bring them together through several strategies. Taxsutra started multiple WhatsApp groups where tax professionals and tax managers could interact and solve one another's doubts. Taxsutra's moderators would share links of relevant court rulings and encourage members to reply to vexing questions. On its portal, it introduced a dedicated page called 'Experts' Corner', where tax experts presented their opinions on complicated issues in tax litigation. A person did not need a subscription to access the high-end content shared by experts.

Tax consultants, whether advocates and chartered accountants, are not allowed by their professional bodies to advertise their services to solicit business. They have to rely on personal networks to locate potential clients. Corporate clients look for professionals with expertise in certain domains. Managers in these corporate houses usually reach out to super-specialists in these areas through personal networks. By bringing together the small but dispersed community of tax experts through its WhatsApp groups, Taxsutra started developing a structured network. The Experts' Corner allowed consultants to showcase their work and their insights of business law to managers in corporate houses. Managers in corporate houses benefited from the high-quality articles from professionals. Even tax officers (officers employed by tax departments and judges in tax tribunals) benefited from these insights. In due course, Taxsutra also started organising webinars and masterclasses on specialised subjects. Consultants would offer to give lectures free-of-cost, as this would increase their visibility. At the same time, viewers were ready to pay to participate in the webinars due to their high quality.

Over time, Taxsutra has become a platform for three groups of customers to connect with one another – tax consultants, tax managers in firms and tax officers. It follows a hybrid business strategy – a pipeline business in its subscription-based content, and a platform business that connects tax experts through WhatsApp groups, Experts' Corner and webinars.

The offer to publish my book meant that Taxsutra was offering me a reach that no traditional publisher could. Taxsutra had data on every tax professional's areas of interest and knew who would purchase what. It could push my books to a wide range of professionals without incurring any marketing expense. By partnering with a traditional publisher, Taxsutra outsourced those functions of publishing of which it did not have any expertise and concentrated on harnessing the core strengths of the Taxsutra platform.

A network becomes more valuable to users as more users join it. This is called 'network effects', and it is the single most powerful driver of value in the digital economy. The earliest known reference to network effects as we see in the digital world was in 1908 in an annual report of the American Telephone & Telegraph Company (AT&T). The telephone was a revolutionary invention of its time. But the first telephone that was supplied was useless. It could not be used to communicate with anyone – because there was no one else to connect to. In fact, the only way a marketer could have sold the first telephone was to give it away for free. When a second user was added, the value of the telephone increased, as the two users could phone each other. When a third user was added, it enhanced the value of the network – while the third user found some utility from being part of the network, the first and second user also experienced enhanced utility. The AT&T annual report of 1908 observed, 'A telephone – without a connection at the other end of the line – is not even a toy or a scientific instrument. It is one of the most useless things in the world. Its value depends on the connection with the other telephone – and increases with the number of connections.'[20]

In 1980, Robert Metcalfe, a co-inventor of the Ethernet, took this idea forward by proposing that the value of a network increases in proportion to the square of the number of connected users. That is, the value of a network is a function of n^2, where n is the number of connected users. Metcalfe's proposition was only indicative of the value of a network and was not a deterministic formula. However, it went on to be called Metcalfe's Law. An empirical backing for this theory was lacking until, in 2013, Dutch researchers presented an analysis of European internet usage patterns over a long period of time and concluded that value increases with the number of connected users, but differently for different network sizes. For small networks, the value increases roughly in proportion to n^2, while in large networks, the value increases roughly in proportion to $n\log n$.[21] In both cases, we see a non-linear rise in the value of a network as membership rises.

Metcalfe's law is a theory (not a law) that holds true in many (but not all) cases. Broadly speaking, there are two kinds of network effects – direct network effects and indirect network effects. Direct network effects result from interaction of users on the same side of the platform. In Facebook's case, for example, direct network effects result from intense interaction of users. Indirect network effects result from interactions of users on two sides of a platform. Ecommerce companies are typical examples of indirect network effects. They have buyers and sellers as the two sides of a two-sided market. Each new buyer adds value to all the sellers on the platform, because now each seller is linked to one more prospective customer on the platform. Each new seller adds value to all buyers on the platform. Flipkart relies on both direct and indirect network effects. Prospective buyers interacting with prospective sellers on Flipkart leads to indirect network effects, while buyers reading reviews and ratings of other buyers lead to direct network effects. Direct networks are known to have stronger effects than indirect networks.

Two important consequences of network effects are 'stickiness' and 'crowding out'. As a network grows beyond a critical size, the value of connections from the network outweighs the cost of remaining in the network. As a result, users tend to stick around, and this stickiness acts as a defence for the network against competitors. For example, consider two social networking apps in a hypothetical school community whose networks are represented by Figure 2.1 and Figure 2.2. If new students have to join one of the apps, which would they select? They would prefer the app in Figure 2.1 because they can connect with more classmates on this app and get more feed, campus news and user updates on this network. The bigger a network, more is its utility for a new user. Further, an existing user of the app in Figure 2.1 will have a tendency to stay with the app and not switch to the app in Figure 2.2 even if the app in Figure 2.2 has a better user interface. Over time, the users in the network in Figure 2.2 will find it more useful to shift to the first network even if the second app has a better user interface. This is how smaller networks are crowded out by a large network (of course, the prediction may not come true if the app in Figure 2.1 malfunctions or does not add functionalities over time). Because of network effects, platform economics has a natural propensity to produce monopolies. And with monopoly status, comes market power.

Figure 2.1: Social networking app A

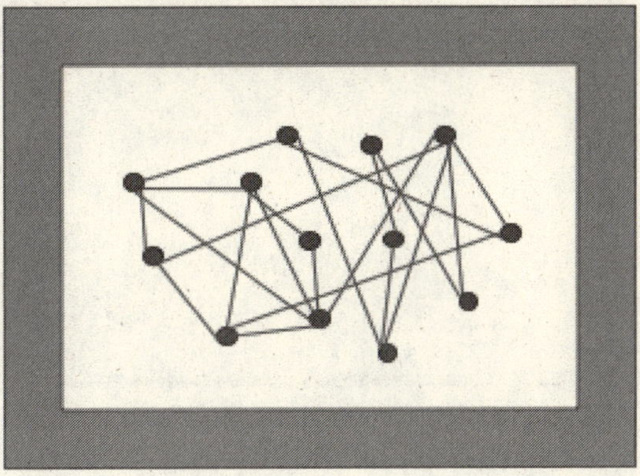

Figure 2.2: Social networking app B

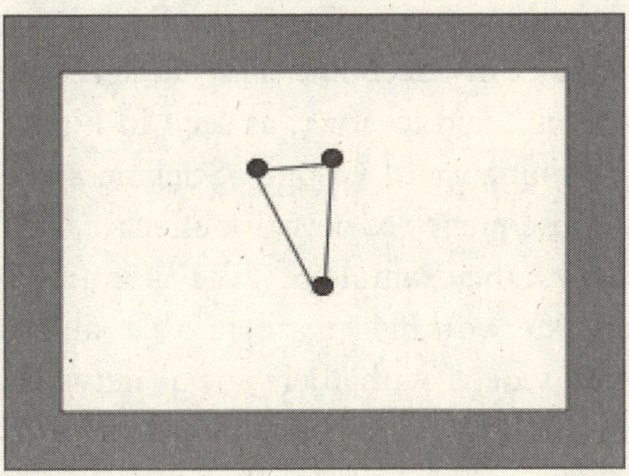

Figure 2.3: Market share of social media portals

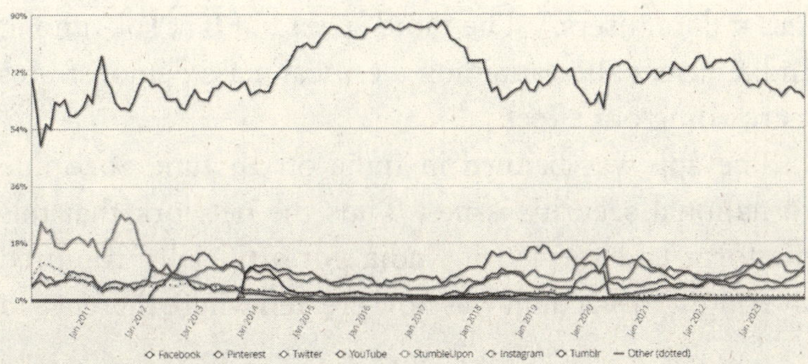

Source: Statcounter

Figure 2.4: Market share of search engines (June 2009 to November 2023)

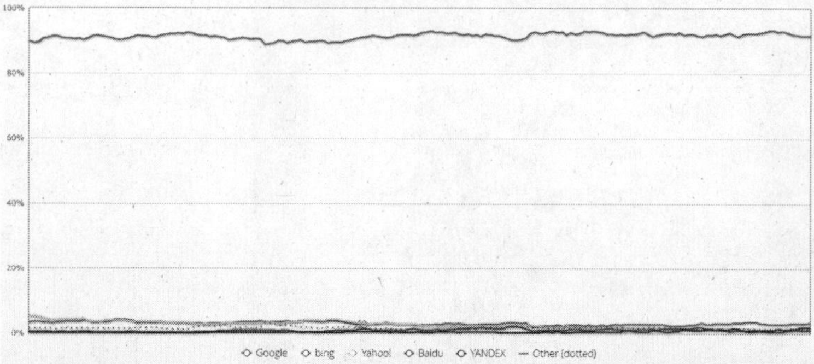

Source: Statcounter

This consequence has been seen in many cases in real life. For example, the market share of social networking portals in India from 2010 to 2023, as seen in Figure 2.3, shows a clear dominance of Facebook. The market share of search engines from 2009 to 2023, as seen in Figure 2.4, shows a clear dominance of Google. Stickiness and crowding out as a consequence of network effects can be best demonstrated with the example of TikTok in India. TikTok is a social networking platform that allows users to share short videos with their social network. Introduced globally in 2017, a substantial chunk of its global growth came from India until early 2020. By that time it had captured 85–90 per cent of India's market for short-form video and was estimated to have garnered 120 million users.[22] The rapid spread of TikTok among Indian users after attaining a critical mass demonstrates a crowding out effect.

The app was banned in India on 29 June 2020 due to national security issues. Thus the network that this platform had formed in India got artificially ruptured overnight. A vacuum was now created where there was a sticky network earlier, a vacuum that competitors would soon fill. A survey in October 2020 by the consultancy firm Redseer found that after it was banned, 40 per cent of its market in India was captured by homegrown start-ups like MX TakaTak, Josh, Moj, Chingari and Mitron.[23] The race to capture TikTok's market involved high stakes – MX TakaTak is backed by Times Internet and Tencent, while Josh is backed by Google and Microsoft and Moj is owned by ShareChat. These two platforms quickly inducted erstwhile users of TikTok into their user base.

A repeat survey by Redseer in April 2021 found that 97 per cent of TikTok's market share had been captured by homegrown start-ups. The survey revealed that users were satisfied with the new platforms they had joined and did not want to go back to TikTok. Users in metro cities found the performance of the new apps they had joined to be at par with TikTok, while users in Tier 1 cities were happy with the app they had joined because their favourite influencers from TikTok had joined it.[24]

Competitors of TikTok had scant chance of success as long as it was ticking. TikTok's network effects were strong and sticky. Its dominant network had crowded out all competitors. But once TikTok stopped, many new start-ups sprouted overnight to seize its network. Time will tell if one of these platforms will dominate the entire market and crowd out all others.

Because network effects have a natural tendency to create monopolies, many business commentators say that it is the 'winner takes all' phenomenon in platform business.[25] After intense rounds of dog fights, one platform company dominates the market for a single service, and all competitors perish. However, this view is an over-generalisation. There are many kinds of networks, and business strategists have now realised that not all networks lead to the desired network effects; not all networks are sticky or crowd out competition. More specifically, there are strong network effects and there are weak network effects. When network effects are weak, the risk of failure of large networks is high. We will revisit this issue in the next chapter when we discuss how to differentiate between platforms.

Volume without Mass

In the book *Platform Scale*, platform evangelist Sangeet Paul Choudary states that scaling up start-ups massively that we have come to see in recent times, does not offer any product or service; it only builds larger platforms on which users can create and exchange value. But a logical consequence of the crowding out effect is that platforms have no option but to scale. While 'winner takes all' is not always true, it is true in most situations. There are three options for a platform: (a) Become the dominant network in a market/community or (b) Sell your network to the competitor owning the dominant network and exit or (c) Perish. To become the dominant network, or to own a network that would be valued by competitors, the platform needs to scale rapidly.

A platform business with mass cannot scale rapidly. By mass I mean physical business processes.[26] Digital services can be scaled at breakneck pace, but this is not the case with physical goods and services. Further, digital services can be expanded to cover more consumers without any increase in marginal cost. Once a mobile app's features have been developed for *n* users, its services can be provided free of cost to (n+1)th user. This is not the case for physical services. Scaling up physical business processes takes time. Since scaling up is a priority for survival, platform businesses tend to have volume without mass. Much like humans, they cannot afford to put on weight if they intend to win the race.

In its growth stage, Ola was strictly a ride hailing app. Its main activity was connecting drivers and riders. After developing a dominance in the Indian market for ride hailing, it started manufacturing electric vehicles. Its move into the physical process of manufacturing electric vehicles will complement its ride hailing services, and it may soon induce drivers on the Ola app to buy cabs from it. But had it packaged its app-based services to cab drivers with physical car sales in the initial phase, it could not have grown at the pace it did.

Platforms Don't Always Have Competitive Advantage

Until now, in this chapter, I appear to have eulogised platforms as being more potent forces of value creation than pipelines. They have a definite competitive advantage when they use connections to remove intermediaries and gatekeepers from the picture. But in many cases they do not have a clear competitive advantage over pipelines. A good example is the case of online grocery start-ups, specifically BigBasket, DMart and JioMart.

Building a platform model around grocery is pretty challenging because grocery is a low margin business. A platform in this segment would be a three-sided model connecting the seller, the buyer and the delivery person. The buyer is very sensitive to prices, as they can alternatively go to the neighbourhood kirana (mom-and-pop) store to buy groceries. Sellers are also sensitive to prices because of the low profit margins. The delivery person has to be paid more than what food delivery persons are paid, because groceries are heavier and hence require more work to deliver.

BigBasket started an online grocery business in 2011. Its business model was a pipeline consisting of large and small warehouses that procured and stored groceries. When a buyer placed an order on the BigBasket app, delivery persons hired by the company delivered the groceries at the buyer's doorstep. Being a typical pipeline, it could maximise its profits by optimising the supply chain and reducing cost. However, the company continued to make losses from inception and booked a loss of 12.4 per cent in FY 2019–20.[27] This kind of performance is not considered good for a traditional business, because it has little chance in the future to earn super-profits to recoup the accumulated losses.[28]

Probably DMart realised this, for it was known to focus on the bottom line. DMart ran an offline supermarket chain in parts of West and South India. If BigBasket carried mass in the form of warehouses and delivery staff, DMart was obese – it owned the land on which it built its supermarkets (most supermarkets take land on lease). Due to acute competition from online grocery delivery companies, it decided to start an online grocery business called DMart Ready. A customer could place orders with DMart Ready and pick up the groceries from a kiosk owned by DMart in the neighbourhood.

The customer could also get home delivery of groceries for a fee. Unlike BigBasket, JioMart or Grofers, it did not do free home delivery, whatever be the order size.[29]

Unlike BigBasket and DMart, Reliance JioMart made a game-plan to harness the power of platforms. It planned to connect kirana stores and customers through the JioMart app. A customer could place an order for groceries on the app. JioMart would forward the order to a nearby kirana store having the necessary stock and the kirana store would make the delivery. This is a typical volume-without-mass business. JioMart made connections but did not take up the responsibility for cumbersome physical processes. The delivery of heavy but low value groceries is the most challenging part in an online grocery business, but JioMart dodged this part by involving kiranas.

But then, kirana stores do not need a mobile app to connect with people in the neighbourhood. Since time immemorial, they have seamlessly connected with customers in the neighbourhood. The neighbourhood is a physical platform on which they have built familiarity with people. Practically, in this case, the app did not do much by way of improving connections and removing intermediaries or gatekeepers. What value did the app provide to bring kirana stores on-board? Which problem of kirana stores was it solving? The Ken reported in May 2021 that this business was not working out as planned and that kirana stores were not keen to on-board the JioMart platform.[30]

What JioMart was trying with kirana stores was not new. A start-up by the name of Peppertap had tried it in 2014 and had even raised upwards of US$ 50 million in funding. It connected local grocery stores with consumers but did not take responsibility of maintaining any inventory. This was a pure platform model. The company offered discounts from its own funds in order to on-board consumers.[31] But they had to perpetually offer discounts to keep consumers faithful; the platform was not sticky enough as grocery stores and grocery consumers in the same neighbourhood did not need the platform to network. However, JioMart did not give up and kept exploring ways to harness the power of networks. It focused on strengthening its non-grocery offerings, closed down quick commerce grocery delivery service that it called JioMart Express[32] and introduced several innovations. In 2022, it partnered with WhatsApp and started offering an end-to-end shopping experience to customers on WhatsApp. Partnership with a much more entrenched platform with strong network effects, and restructuring of business, worked wonders for JioMart, and it managed to increase the customer base of ecommerce vertical by 9 times in a year's time.[33] JioMart has survived and flourished because it resorted to something called 'network bridging', which we will discuss in detail in Chapter 3.

There are other situations in which platforms do not provide a competitive advantage over pipelines. To identify such situations, we need to first identify the actors it seeks to on-board onto its platform. In an *n*-sided market, there are *n* set of actors. Then we need to ask some basic questions – what is the platform offering to the different actors? Which problem of theirs is the platform trying to solve? Is the solution incremental or transformational? If buyers of any goods or service are concentrated or easily accessible to sellers, then the sellers would prefer to invest in their own distribution channel rather than on-board a third-party platform. But if the sellers are small and the market is fragmented, sellers would not be willing to invest in a costly distribution channel. In such situations, platforms provide a solution by aggregating the services of different sellers.[34] Sangeet Paul Choudary has predicted three factors that drive disruption by platforms: (a) Platforms will displace high cost gatekeepers with meritocratic crowds, (b) Platforms will aggregate disconnected players in fragmented industries and (c) Platforms will unlock new value from spare resources and user-generated content.[35] I predict that when a platform does not provide one of these three solutions, it does not have a competitive advantage over pipelines.

This chapter presented the contrast between platform business models and traditional business, and has demonstrated why value creation increases exponentially with expansion in platform businesses. It also explained the vexing question of why platforms bleed and incur heavy losses in their start-up years. In the next chapter, we will try to differentiate between the kinds of platform companies and see which of these are good bets for investing.

3

Platform Power

Treebo's founders were in for an existential crisis one fine day in March 2017. Treebo gives hotel rooms on rent, and reaches out to its customers through online platforms. It received a good number of customers through the MakeMyTrip portal. On that fateful day, MakeMyTrip had removed all listings of Treebo from its portal.[1] Treebo's founders and managers, I imagine, frantically reached out to MakeMyTrip management and pleaded to be allowed to use the portal to connect to prospective customers.

Treebo Hotels is a Bengaluru-based company that provides franchising services to budget hotels in India. Small budget hotels get some advantages from the Treebo brand, such as access to the company's sales and marketing expertise, standardised guest services, and synergy benefits from being part of a hotel chain. Officially called Rubtub Solutions Private Limited, the company faced what could be called a 'black swan event' without much exaggeration when MakeMyTrip delisted Treebo hotels from its portal. The delisting adversely affected Treebo's business and profits,[2] and the company subsequently alleged that this was the retaliation for not capitulating to certain threats made by MakeMyTrip.

MakeMyTrip is an online travel agency that connects users with airlines and hotels. A hotelier who accepts the portal's terms and conditions can list their rooms on the portal. A user can book rooms in listed hotels through the MakeMyTrip portal. The platform company went public with an IPO in NASDAQ in 2010, and remains a leading online portal for hotel bookings in India. In 2016, it acquired Goibibo, another leading portal for hotel bookings, which significantly increased its network in the Indian market.

Treebo stated that MakeMyTrip–Goibibo had a dominant market share of about 63 per cent among online hotel booking portals.[3] This meant that about 63 per cent of prospective customers looking for a hotel in another city, or a resort in a hill station, relied on MakeMyTrip for their bookings. If a hotel was not on MakeMyTrip, it would not have access to these customers. After acquiring Goibibo in 2016, MakeMyTrip had approached Treebo with an offer – that it would make a significant investment in Treebo in exchange for Treebo listing itself exclusively on the MakeMyTrip portal.[4]

Treebo said that during negotiations MakeMyTrip's officials issued direct threats – that they would remove Treebo from their portal. Negotiations broke down in March 2017 and MakeMyTrip removed Treebo from its portal within days. Left without any choice to reach the customers who bought rooms on the MakeMyTrip portal, Treebo approached MakeMyTrip with a plea to let it access the portal. MakeMyTrip placed some conditions that Treebo needed to fulfil to get back access. The first condition was that Treebo would not list its hotel rooms in major Indian cities on Booking.com and Paytm, two competitors of MakeMyTrip. The second condition was that prices quoted on any other platform by Treebo hotels would not be lower than prices quoted on MakeMyTrip.

Under pressure due to the loss from the delisting, Treebo agreed to the conditions, although it felt they were unjust and unfair. MakeMyTrip allowed Treebo to list its hotels again after about six months of remaining blocked. This whole affair showed that Treebo was fundamentally on shaky grounds, and more importantly, that its business was dependent on gatekeepers like MakeMyTrip.[5]

Gatekeepers can favour a competitor and marginalise a firm. Bureaucrats and politicians enjoy wide powers and low accountability in many countries and are often seen as gatekeepers in traditional businesses such as civil contracts and real estate. Such gatekeeping leads to a culture of favouritism, red-tapism and rent-seeking – some of the malice we often see in less–developed countries. Deregulation and free markets are often seen as panacea to such evils. But as the ordeal of Treebo shows, the kind of power that bureaucrats and politicians wield in a heavily regulated market is wielded by dominant companies in free markets.

Treebo's ordeals did not seem to end. In less than six months, MakeMyTrip terminated its deal with Treebo and kicked its hotels out of its portal. This time, it entered into a strategic partnership with Oyo Rooms, another hotel chain providing franchising services to budget hotels, and thus a direct competitor of Treebo. Shunting out Treebo Hotels and Fab Hotels (another franchising chain in the budget hotel segment) was a specific clause of the commercial agreement between MakeMyTrip and Oyo Rooms.[6]

Misusing market dominance isn't legal, but it is definitely not criminal. Treebo approached the Competition Commission of India (CCI) after being delisted from MakeMyTrip's portal a second time. CCI is a watchdog responsible for identifying and remedying uncompetitive practices. Regulators like CCI play an important role in free markets. A free market works freely when every market participant follows rules of the market and does not game it. But gaming does happen in the real world, resulting in market failures, and thus the need for referees. One key reason for market failures is market power, and in India CCI plays the role of a referee to monitor misuse of market power.

CCI promptly took up Treebo's case and investigated its allegations. Three years after the delisting, in March 2021, CCI directed MakeMyTrip to list hotel properties of Treebo and Fab Hotels on its portal 'with immediate effect' thus bringing to end Treebo's ordeal. For now. The losses to Treebo in terms of opportunity cost, loss of customers and sentiments of franchisee hotels during the two periods of disruption in 2017 and 2018–2021 is incalculable. In October 2022, CCI took a final decision in this matter and imposed a monetary penalty on MakeMyTrip and Oyo at the rate of 5 per cent of the relevant turnovers, amounting to ₹223 crore for MakeMyTrip and ₹169 crore for Oyo.[7]

Conclusions of the Competition Commission of India in the Case

1. Dominance
    a. MakeMyTrip operates in the market for 'online intermediation services for booking of hotels in India'; investigation has found it having the highest market share in the segment.
    b. Both user groups positively value the presence of more users on the other side of the platform, as it creates higher visibility and potential sales (for hotels) and wider variety and options (for consumers).
    c. Barriers to entry and expansion informs the state of competitiveness in a market. The last entry in this market was by HappyEasyGo in 2017, and it had a mere 0.2% market share in 2019–20.
    d. Network effects play a pivotal role in dominance assessment. MakeMyTrip offers several benefits and features, which coupled with its market position has resulted in network effects. Such network effects also create insurmountable entry barriers for existing as well as potential market participants
2. Denial of Market Access
    a. MakeMyTrip is a gateway for online hotel booking, which constitutes an important access route for independent hotels to reach the end-consumers.
    b. Denial of access to MakeMyTrip, an important channel of distribution, through foreclosure adversely affected competition in the market.
    c. Equitable access to a dominant online intermediation on fair terms is necessary for the functioning of businesses which rely on such intermediaries to reach the end-consumers.

Source: https://www.cci.gov.in/images/antitrustorder/en/odrer1666182873.pdf

In the previous chapter, I delved into business models to differentiate between traditional companies and platform companies which have thrived with the evolution of the digital economy. In this chapter, I will discuss different kinds of platforms to identify the ones which have the potential to make super-profits for their shareholders in the future. In the next chapter, I will present the vulnerabilities of platform companies.

As we had seen in the last chapter, digital markets tend to be naturally dominated by a monopoly or duopoly due to network effects. The dominance of companies which enjoy a high market share comes with many perks. Dominant companies can use their *scale*, their *scope* and their *network* to earn super-profits for their shareholders. Such dominance, often referred as 'corporate concentration', is often seen as a social and economic problem because dominance leads to inefficiency and inequity in the market and is often prone to misuse. It eventually leads to market failure. But for shareholders, dominance is a good thing. A dominant company can use its powers over its business partners, its competitors and its customers to earn rents – which ultimately benefits the shareholders.

And since the digital world promotes corporate concentration through network effects, we will have to live with it. However, not every company with a large network sustains and makes super-profits in the long run. There are features that can help us identify the ones which will succeed and go on to dominate the digital world. These features are important for everyone who wants to make intelligent investments. Before discussing them, we will first take a detour to analyse the traditional economy to understand why corporate concentration leads to super-profits.

Market Power

Consider this hypothesis – larger firms make more profits than smaller firms. This is a broad generalisation which an economist would frown upon. We can list many exceptions to this hypothesis. Nor does the hypothesis get any strong backing from concepts. Textbook microeconomics informs us that *economies of scale* kick in as production increases, because the per unit cost of production decreases. This leads to lower costs and higher profits. Large size also means cheaper procurement (because the raw material is sourced in bulk), cheaper technology (the same technology licensed from the owner can be used for more production) and cheaper finance. But when a firm becomes very large, *diseconomies of scale* kick in. Managing a large firm without a bureaucracy is difficult. Bureaucracies mean inefficiency and slow decision making. Mismanagement leads to wastage and larger overheads, and thus costs increase.

Chief executives have managed to cope with the issue of *diseconomies of scale* to an extent by using the advances in information and communication technology (ICT). An enterprise resource planning (ERP) software (such as SAP) collects critical data across the supply chain and feeds it to the managers. Top management can distil key insights from this data and specifically identify where pilferages or wastages are taking place, or the business processes that are working inefficiently.

At the same time, there are many competitive advantages of size which textbooks do not discuss. One is the synergy benefits that arise when different business units interact. The best practices that one unit has developed by 'learning by doing' processes can be replicated in other units. Two business units in complementary businesses can promote each other's products to customers. Customer relationships established by one business unit can be easily leveraged by other units. Trade secrets of one unit can be utilised by another. Business synergy is a key motivator for large merger and acquisition (M&A) activities and the amounts involved in them have risen hugely over the past few decades.[8]

Another advantage that size bestows is in the norms which a customer may set. Customers looking to execute a turnkey project or a large business transformation look for a contractor of a certain minimum size. Not every company can deliver a large project on time, and lack of expertise on the part of the contractor can adversely affect the customer's affairs. Government tenders place numerous conditions on awarding contracts, which invariably include a base minimum sales turnover, years of experience in executing such contracts and existing capacity to execute the contract. While large firms can apply for small contracts, small firms cannot apply for large contracts.

Government regulations can also provide many competitive advantages to large firms. Intellectual property rights (IPR) are monopoly rights granted by the government to a company for an innovation. The company could utilise the IPR for generating monopoly profits during the tenure of the rights. Since there is no competition, the company could charge high prices to customers and get super-profits. Lobbying helps large corporates to influence government rules and regulations. For example, when copyright law was first codified in the

US, IPR was available to the owner for only 14 years. By the time the first Mickey Mouse cartoon was released by Disney in 1928, the copyright period had increased to 56 years. The copyright over Mickey Mouse should have expired in 1984. However, Disney lobbied for increasing the copyright duration to protect its monopoly rights over the Mickey Mouse cartoon character. In 1976, the copyright tenure was retrospectively increased to 75 years, and again, in 1998 it was retrospectively increased to 95 years. Disney now has copyright over Mickey Mouse till 2023.[9]

IP laws are among a group of business laws that a corporate group has to navigate, and large corporations can hire the best to lobby for rules to favour them. Interestingly, even though tax laws apply equally to large and small firms in theory, large firms can structure their business in such a way that they declare most of their profits in tax havens, thus legitimately minimising their tax liability. Lower effective tax means higher profits to be distributed to shareholders.

Dominance in a market opens up many other avenues of earning super-profits. A certain market can be a monopoly (dominated by one company), a duopoly (dominated by two companies), or an oligopoly (dominated by a handful of companies). Dominant companies can charge a toll (or a tax) just to access the market if they control it. For instance, MasterCard and Visa dominate the entire global market for credit card payment systems. This is because they control the core infrastructure used by merchants and bankers for card transactions. This position of dominance has enabled the two companies to levy onerous fees on merchants, which is nothing but an invisible tax.[10] A dominant company can use predatory pricing to destroy smaller competitors to achieve control over the market. Once it destroys competition and gets control, it can charge higher prices from customers and demand goods and services at lower prices from vendors. Predatory pricing also discourages new competitors from entering the market.

Thus, corporate concentration leads to market power and there are multiple avenues of using this market power to gain super-profits.[11] Corporate concentration and super-profits have been positively correlated in many studies in recent years. *The Economist* notes, 'A small number of giant companies are … on the march, tightening their grip on global markets, merging with each other to get even bigger, and enjoying vast profits.'[12] Profits of a firm comprise returns on capital, labour, other endowments and depend on the risks taken. Once the returns on these factors are removed from the profits, what remains is economic rent or super-profit. The Trade and Development Report 2018 of UNCTAD states, 'Increased market concentration and rising markups have become commonplace across many sectors and economies, with rent-seeking behaviour dominating at the top of the corporate food chain. These trends have inevitably extended across borders.'[13]

In India, a few researchers have found high levels of corporate concentration in some sectors.[14] A working paper of 2019 released by the Institute for Studies in Industrial Development, New Delhi, revealed findings of a study of twenty-nine sub-sectors in manufacturing and found high levels of corporate concentration in seven of them.[15] However, I could not find any research report on the Indian market that showed relative profitability of big and small companies over time for a specific sector. So I teamed up with Professor Suranjali Tandon of the National Institute of Public Finance and Policy (NIPFP), a Delhi-based autonomous research institute of the Government of India, to crunch corporate data and find a link between size and profitability.

In our study, we took the whole dataset of company data from a public database for four sectors, namely, software development, Information Technology Enabled Services (ITES), pharmaceuticals and steel.[16] We found that the number of companies in each of the sectors having a market share of more than 1 per cent was low, but their share in total sales for the sector was high (Figures 3.1 and 3.2). After iterating with different percentages we found that 1 per cent would be fairly representative across industries as a threshold at which profit margins above and below the threshold become incomparable. So we decided on 1 per cent as the threshold to brand big and small companies.

Our results were revealing because they showed a clear difference in average profits of companies having more than 1 per cent market share and companies having less than 1 per cent market share. As can be seen from Figure 3.3, the gap in profitability was significant and consistent in a 20-year period from 2000 to 2019. This is clear evidence linking profitability to market share of firms.

Another evidence linking profitability to market share was published as a working paper by the Mumbai-based Indira Gandhi Institute of Developmental Research (IGIDR) months before the results of our research were published. The paper concludes that large and group companies are more profitable than small and standalone companies.[17] Interestingly, this research identified the increase in profitability due to cost efficiency and managed to isolate the delta profitability attributable to market power. The paper concludes that higher profitability of large companies is due to market power.

Figure 3.1: Number of companies in four sectors with market share more than 1 per cent (based on data from Prowess database)

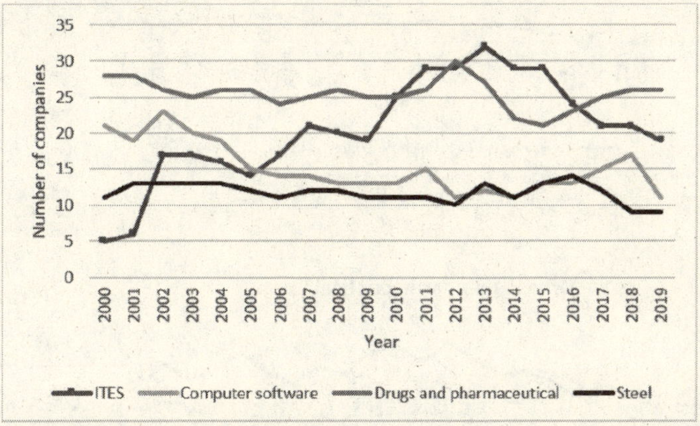

Source: Swain and Tandon (2020)

Figure 3.2: Cumulative market share of companies with more than 1 per cent market share in respective markets (based on data from Prowess database)

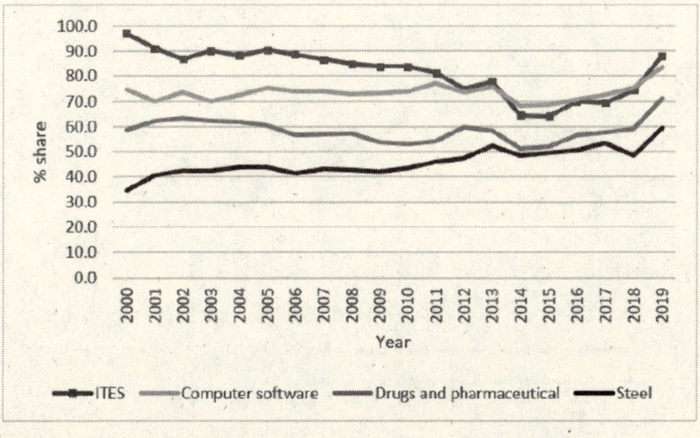

Source: Swain and Tandon (2020)

Figure 3.3: Average profitability of companies with more than 1 per cent market share and those with less than 1 per cent market share in different markets

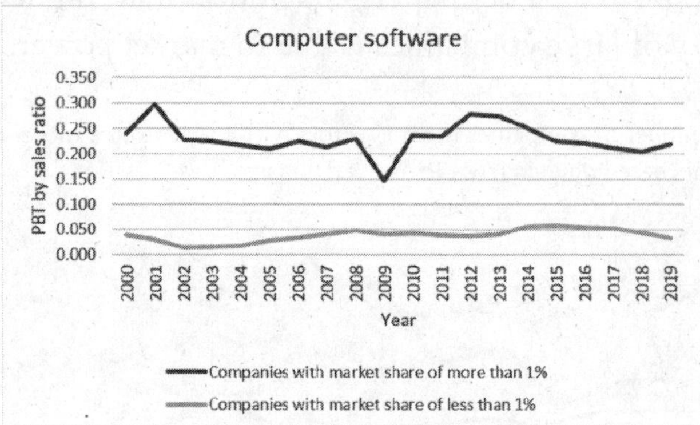

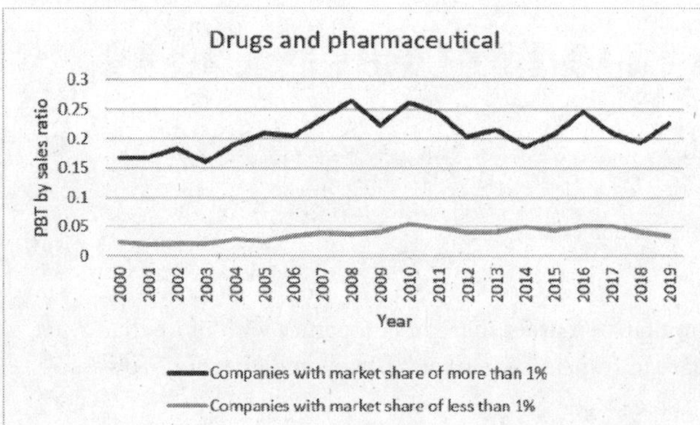

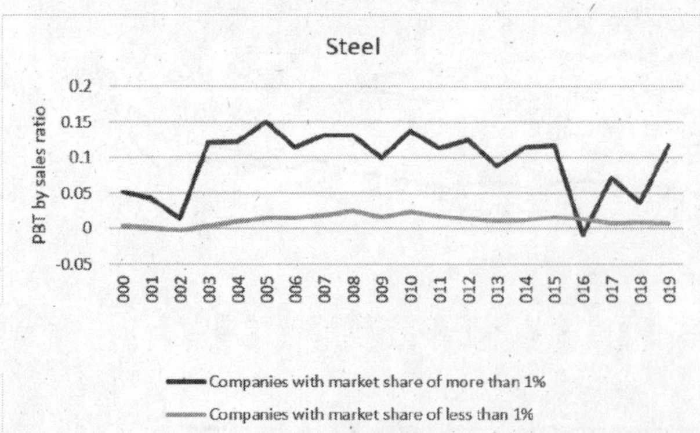

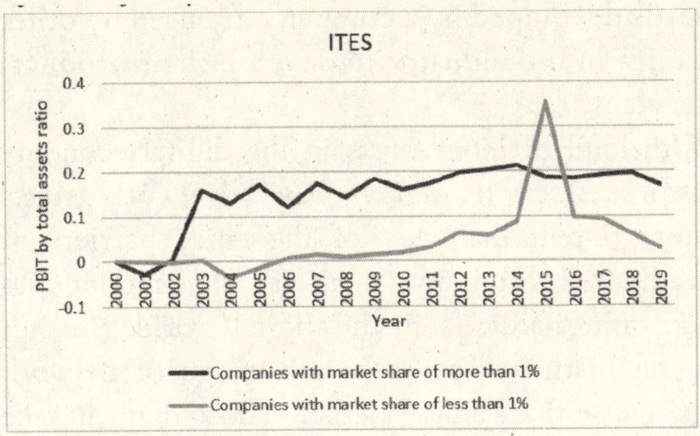

Source: Swain and Tandon (2020)

Companies with market power have the best chances of producing profits and giving good returns to shareholders in the long term. They are best placed to raise entry barriers and control competition in their respective industry and may also enjoy a large influence in other industries as well if they play the role of a gatekeeper.

Another logical conclusion from this discussion is that entry barriers and anti-competitive strategies raise shareholder value. But a negative image can put off conscientious investors, so investment advisers often use positive words like 'competitive advantage' and 'moats' to present the point. A moat, as the word suggests, is an entry barrier to competition. A *cost moat* results from economies of scale and cost efficiency. It can also appear if the cost of switching to another product is high for its customers. A *cultural moat* results from strong brand identification, which breeds brand loyalty. A *resource moat* is a special status or license or IP granted by the government. A *standards moat* develops when standards developed by a company are used by other companies in the industry to develop their products and services.

A fifth kind of moat exists in the digital economy – network effects or *network moat*. Network effects are more potent than any of the entry barriers of the traditional economy. That is why monopolies develop quite naturally in the digital world. But not all digital platforms can take advantage of network effects. Those that cannot, perish. Those that can take advantage of network effects either grow to become a monopoly, or profitably merge into one. If we can identify the companies that develop the most durable and unassailable network moats, we will know which companies will grow to dominate markets in the digital world. These companies may be incurring losses now, but they will more than make up later with super-profits and rent collections.

Research has revealed some factors that affect the fate of networks. To drive the point that large networks do not necessarily translate into dominance, Feng Zhu and Marco Iansiti, at the Harvard Business School, narrate the story of Didi, a ride-sharing app company in China.[18] In 2016, this company attained a monopoly status in China after acquiring a domestic rival and pushing Uber out of the country. After squeezing out competitors, it reduced discounts and started increasing its margins. But just when Didi was turning profitable, a new competitor entered the business in Shanghai. This competitor did not charge any commission from drivers for the first three months and later charged a much lower commission than Didi. Riders and drivers flocked towards this new service. Shortly after, a few other competitors entered the market in different cities and offered deep discounts. As a result, Didi was forced to reduce the commission it charged from the drivers.

Zhu and Iansiti reason that *network clustering* has an important role to play in determining the strength of network effects. Companies like Didi and Uber connect drivers and riders locally in a city. They form multiple small clusters at the level of cities. Clusters of two different cities are isolated from each other. Hyperlocal apps such as MyGate (an app to manage activities of housing societies) and SuprDaily (an app to order milk and other perishables) form even smaller clusters. In contrast, Facebook forms large clusters connecting users from across a country and also users from multiple countries. Figure 3.4 shows a representative contrast between fragmented network clusters such as that of Uber and Didi, and unified clusters such as that of Facebook.

Figure 3.4: A representation of two different network structures

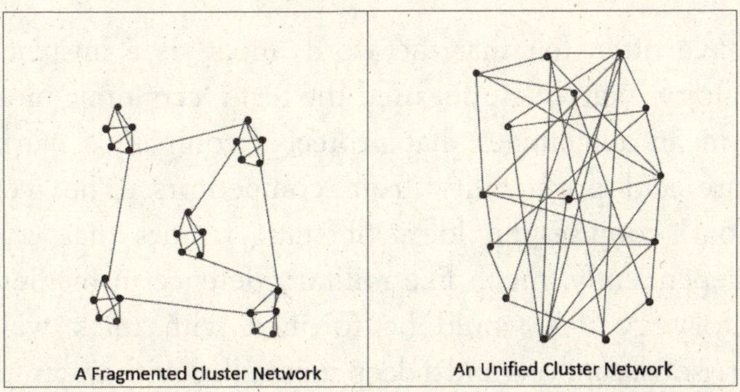

Source: Based on Zhu and Iansiti (2019)

Another challenge that ride sharing companies face is that of *multi-homing*. Multi-homing happens when users connect with each other through multiple platforms at the same time. For example, I have installed both Uber and Ola, and I check the price and wait time on both apps every time I want to book a taxi. Back in 2014, I had three apps on my phone – Uber, Ola and TaxiForSure. Ola acquired TaxiForSure at a premium in March 2015. I wonder how wise it was for Ola to acquire TaxiForSure at a premium, given that their networks were largely duplicative. Ola's network did not get any synergy benefit from the acquisition, as most users of TaxiForSure were also users of Ola. Not surprisingly, Ola shut down TaxiForSure a year and a half after the takeover.[19]

We have had enough experience with digital networks by now to identify and isolate factors that influence network effects. However, more interesting and also more useful will be factors that increase potency and durability of network effects.

The Flywheel

I have often felt that the word 'moat' is a misplaced analogy. Warren Buffet used the term 'economic moat' to mean advantages that protect a company's market share and profitability from competitors. The word 'moat' conjures up ideas of static factors that work independently, much like military defence in medieval history. A fort would be fortified with thick walls, garrisons, cannons and a deep moat filled with water and crocodiles. All these defences worked independently to slow down an enemy army trying to breach the fort's walls.

But modern warfare is much different. Modern warfare demands close coordination between army, navy, air force, engineering corps and spy agencies. These arms of a unified defence command not only play their own part, but also reinforce each other's strengths. They form a dynamic whole in which parts consistently reinforce each other's efforts.

Network effects strategy needs to be perceived in the same manner – dynamic interaction of many factors reinforcing each other as well as the network. Amazon's network strategy – the Amazon Flywheel – is an apt illustration of this idea. The flywheel, depicted in Figure 3.5, was developed in 2001 by Jeff Bezos as a virtuous cycle and has been improved upon many times over the years by Amazon. The flywheel shows many factors working dynamically to provide positive reinforcements to growth. These factors also provide a positive feedback loop to each other. A flywheel is a much better analogy for business defences than a moat – it depicts dynamism as well as interconnectedness.

Figure 3.5: A representation of the Amazon flywheel

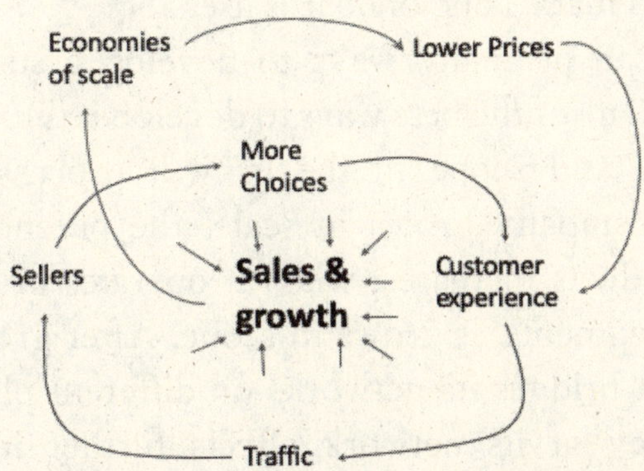

Amazon has been highly invested in the idea of its network as a dynamic virtuous cycle. On the Amazon marketplace, buyers interact with sellers to purchase goods. Buyers also interact with each other through the reviews and ratings section for each product. Buyers also connect with sellers through advertisements. Data collected in all these processes helps Amazon understand buyer preferences, which in turn helps Amazon's own selling affiliates gain insights and expand their business. Taking the idea even further, Amazon is connecting its different networks with each other. This strategy is called *network bridging*.[20] Other tech giants such as Google, Apple and Facebook also follow this strategy.

Rather than look for moats, a prospective investor should look for flywheels. The key question about digital platforms is whether they have a sustainable network or an unsustainable network. A platform with an unsustainable network keeps burning money to maintain the network. If it manages to get investment, it grows; but it will still need to burn money to maintain the network. A platform with a sustainable network, on the other hand, burns money only in the start-up phase – the phase in which it builds its multi-sided market and onboards users.

There can be many ways to develop a sustainable flywheel. One of the best ways to develop it is to manage both scale and scope in the growth process. When a digital company grows in scale, the potency of its network effects increases; when it operates in multiple business segments, it grows in scope. After growing in scope, if it bridges its networks on different platforms, the potency of its network effects further increases. Strong network effects with a large scale provide market power. Market power in one segment helps the company dominate in other business segments as well. All these factors working together increase the durability of the network.

This interplay between scale and scope can be summarised with the stylised example in Table 3.1.

Table 3.1: Interplay between Scale and Scope

Scale + scale = Network Effects	Consider Google, which has its own search engine, Maps and Mail. Google offers the Android operating system free to smartphone sellers. Android connects app developers with users. By doing so, it acts as a platform and develops a network between app developers and users. As it grows in scale, its network gains potency.
Scale + Scope = Network Effects	Google's search engine, Maps and Mail come pre-installed on Android. By doing this, Google is bridging its networks for Google search, Gmail and Google maps with Android's network. This further increases the potency of Android network.
Network Effect + Scale = Dominance	As the network of developers and users grows, Android inches out competition. It gains a dominant position in the market.
Scope + Dominance = Market Power	Android can now use its dominance to promote other products of Google. It controls the terms and conditions on which app developers can sell apps in its Play Store. It is the policeman in the store. Further, developers cannot move to another platform if Android starts charging them more than fair commission. If a third-party application wants to compete with Google's in-house products, Android has the power to block it or bully it.

Scale + Scope + Network Effects + Dominance + Market Power = Durability	Potency and durability are two elements of a sustainable network.

The stylised example in Table 3.1 is based on the substance of a complaint filed with CCI in 2018. This complaint alleged that Google provided licences for its Android OS to phone manufacturers free of cost. However, the licensed version would not contain Google Play Store, the app store that phone users would expect pre-installed on their Android mobile. To get the Play Store app, phone manufacturers have to sign a separate agreement under which Google's entire suite of apps are pre-installed on the Android phone. There is an anti-fragmentation clause in this agreement, mandating that the suite cannot be fragmented to pre-install only Play Store. Along with the Play Store, the phone manufacturer has to pre-install Google's mobile search, Google Maps, Gmail and a host of other Google apps. The complaint alleged that this was the way Google was misusing its dominance to push its products in preference to competitors. The Commission made the following observation when opening investigations:

> The Commission is of the prima facie opinion that mandatory pre-installation of the entire GMS suite … amounts to imposition of an unfair condition on the device manufacturers. ... It also amounts to prima facie leveraging of Google's dominance in Play Store to protect the relevant markets such as

> online general search. ... Mobile search has emerged as a key gateway for users to access information and Android is a key distribution channel for mobile search engines. Search engines exhibit data-driven scale effects. Improvements in search algorithms require sufficient volume of data, which, in turn, needs sufficient volume of queries from users who are increasingly resorting to mobile search. Thus, the impugned conduct of Google may help perpetuate its dominance in the online search market while resulting in denial of market access for competing search apps. ... These aspects warrant a detailed investigation.[21]

A final investigation report released by CCI in September 2021 found that Google's action violated India's competition law in two ways – it imposed unfair conditions on the device manufacturers; and it used its dominance in operating systems for smartphones to dominate the market for other products.[22] Subsequently, on 25 October 2022, CCI imposed a penalty of ₹936.44 crore on Google on grounds of the company 'abusing its dominant position with respect to its Play Store policies', apart from issuing a cease-and-desist order.[23] It also provided Google a timeline to modify its conduct.

It would be interesting to see how antitrust laws evolve to detect and control such practices. For now, it appears that CCI and platform companies are looking at the issue from different angles. While CCI sees a misuse of dominance, platform companies see it as a synergy benefit. Google licenses its operating system to phone manufacturers free of cost not as an act of charity but as a part of its business strategy to gain network effects and use these effects to promote its other products (the freemium model). While CCI sees Google as suppressing competition, Google sees itself as facilitating competition. By providing its operating system free to phone manufacturers, it removes access barriers and promotes competition among phone manufacturers. Its act of giving Android operating system free also reduces the cost of smartphones and makes them more affordable for customers.

Do Digital Platforms Have Any Fundamentals?

The stock market is a strange animal. There are some who believe they can beat the market. Others claim that while everyone tries to beat the market, no one ends up beating the market in the long run. A sobering argument between these two extremes is that investing in stocks of companies with sound fundamentals pays in the long run. We get too much investment advice, probably because everyone following the market has a strong opinion and also because no one can really predict the market. It is too chaotic.

Notwithstanding the unpredictable nature of markets, I often reach out to people with their skin in the game for intelligent predictions. One such person is Mumbai-based Ashish Karan, a former director at the Carlyle Group (a multinational corporation engaged in private equity and alternative asset management). In 2021, amid the pandemic, he left his job, purchased some farmland miles away from Mumbai, in Raigad district, and started poultry farming. His LinkedIn profile says he is 'on a break', but he has been busy chasing chicks (quite literally) and digging a pond at his farm. The good thing is that, away from the hustle of a private equity (PE) firm, he has time to brood.

Karan's key takeaway from his long career as an investor is that you should not miss the big trends of your times. You make money when your investment decisions are in sync with these big trends. One prominent trend of the past decade, according to him, was the large influx of money into companies in developing countries. Interest yield in the bond market had been continuously falling in the developed world, while liquidity had been increasing. To cope with the subprime crisis of 2008, the US Federal Reserve introduced a policy called 'quantitative easing', which basically meant printing more dollars and infusing them into the market. This increased liquidity. Low interest rates and high liquidity meant that fund houses had to invest in riskier assets to be able to give adequate returns to their investors. A lot of these funds were invested in stocks in developing countries like India. While the rise in valuation we saw in the Indian stock market was the result of both company performance and infusion of money from abroad, the major proportion of the increase was because of the money coming from Western countries.

The flow of capital across borders has remained unabated since the subprime crisis. Cross-border financial assets reached US$130 trillion in 2020, which was 153 per cent of world GDP.[24] Intuitively, this is a good thing because developing countries need capital to develop. Foreign investment means more development and more jobs. Karan's point is that foreign money prefers large companies and tech start-ups rather than small and medium-sized enterprises (SMEs), due to which (a) it is cheaper for larger companies to get capital and (b) valuations of large companies and tech start-ups have been expanding.

Karan is especially wary of tech companies whose unit economics does not make sense. Unit economics means direct cost and revenue on a per-unit basis. Let us understand this better from the perspective of a platform. Theoretically, once the digital infrastructure of a platform is ready, the infrastructure can be used millions of times without any additional cost. After the cost in the infrastructure is recouped, the marginal cost for every additional unit transaction is zero. All the revenue that the platform receives is the profit of the platform.

$$\Delta \text{ Profit} = \Delta \text{ Revenue} - \Delta \text{ Cost}$$
$$\Delta \text{ Cost} = 0$$
$$\therefore \Delta \text{ Profit} = \Delta \text{ Revenue}$$

But some of the large tech platforms operating in India today fail the test of unit economics. A tech platform which has picked a substantial mass of users but still fails this test should be red flagged as being unusual.

Coming back to the network as a moat, the nature of the network determines how sustainable a platform is. The key characteristic of a sustainable network is the formation of a virtuous cycle that reinforces the network and helps it grow. Theoretically, once a virtuous cycle kicks in, the network retains its existing users and adds additional users at no additional cost. Hence, a sustainable network also passes the unit economics test. An unsustainable network, on the other hand, would need to incur significant costs to retain users and acquire new users. If the cost of user retention is more than the revenue per user, the network fails the unit economics test.

Hence, unit economics is another way of judging whether a platform has a sustainable network or not. Sustainability of their network is the fundamental base of platform companies. A good thing for retail investors is that they usually come into picture at (or after) the IPO stage. By this time, the company is past its start-up phase and its long-term unit economics can be predicted based on contemporary trends.

While I have been describing the wonders of the platform revolution and the potential it offers towards wealth creation, veterans like Ashish Karan have been wary of the uncertainties surrounding the new digital economy. Platform companies are subject to many significant risks other than market risk. In the next chapter, we will examine the risks and uncertainties affecting platform companies.

4

Platform Vulnerabilities

'Paytm' stands for 'pay through mobile'. The Paytm app started as a digital payment system, but over time morphed into a full stack fintech company – providing banking, ecommerce and financial services through its app. It floated an IPO in 2021 offering its shares at ₹2,150 each. The offer price was based on a valuation by lead bankers Morgan Stanley and Goldman Sachs. The company listed on the stock market on 18 November 2018 at ₹1,560 a share, an erosion of over 27 per cent of the IPO price. The stock then slid down to ₹1,304 on 20 December 2021. A couple of days later, Morgan Stanley's research arm asserted that the stock was undervalued and set a target price of ₹1,875 per share.[1] This confidence did not stop the slide, and Paytm was trading on 22 Jan 2022 at ₹917 – an erosion of over 41 per cent in just two months. The erosion has continued, and as of 20 December 2023, it was trading at ₹622.

A side story to the disheartening performance of Paytm is that of Morgan Stanley. The banker was an investor in Paytm before the IPO. While its research arm was broadcasting confidence in the stock's value, its trading arm was selling off Paytm shares. According to the online portal Moneycontrol, Morgan Stanley sold a substantial portion of its shareholding in Paytm in the October–December quarter of 2021.[2] Business journalist Varun Sood took to social media to state, 'There is something rotten here.' The co-author of an engaging biography on Azim Premji, Sood was usually balanced and reasoned in his writings. So this comment piqued my curiosity, and I asked him directly if he was alleging a billion-dollar MNC of running a pump-and-dump scheme (a stock market manipulation technique in which the manipulator first raises the price of a stock artificially and then disposes its own holding of the stock at the artificially inflated price). Sood told me he did not have a straight answer to my question. Business journos like him are told that the trading arm and the research arm of investment banks do not talk to each other; and yet, he has seen in decades of reporting that the same financial service corporation's research arm puts a rating that is contradictory to the actions taken by the trading arm.

On a first look, there appears to be something rotten here. That one arm of Morgan Stanley acted as the lead banker and arrived at the price at which Paytm went public does not help in making it sound less conspiratorial. But one possible scenario is that different departments within Morgan Stanley valued the shares of Paytm differently. Valuation is not an easy science. In fact, it is more of an art than a science. Even for a traditional company, there are just too many variables a valuer has to assume or estimate. That is why a good valuer provides a range, not a price point, and substantiates the range using both market comparables and cash flow projections.

The challenges in valuation are amplified significantly in the case of tech companies. There are multiple reasons for this. The printing press took more than three centuries to diffuse across the globe and be used widely. It took the world less than three decades to adopt the innovation of mobile phones. Experts in their respective fields are still coming to terms with the platform revolution, and there is an asymmetry in appreciating this revolution between the geeks and the others. For example, accounting standards have evolved organically over time and have been completely attuned to the traditional economy. A major development in the past thirty years has been the disproportionate share of intangibles in generation of business profits. Boards for making accounting standards have tried a patchwork approach to handling intangibles and haven't even tried to develop fresh accounting procedures to record financials of digital companies. Another issue is that of economists. Economists are divided in their interpretation of cryptos and platforms. Ideally, adherents of a scientific field of study should not have views that are polar opposite of each other. Economist and columnist Swaminathan S. Anklesaria Aiyar, whose famous column 'Swaminomics' made economic events easy and fun to comprehend, denounces tech stocks and said:

> I remember college boys plunging into dotcom companies in 1999 and making quick fortunes. ... That madness has now come back. College students are once again making money in markets, above all in cryptocurrencies. Youngsters who cannot pass college exams think they are geniuses because they plunged

> early into bitcoin, ethereum, cardano and hundreds of other cryptos that look like pure con games to me.[3]

Aiyar is quite fixated on the idea of passing exams as an indicator of competence. That gives some comfort to the likes of me who slogged for years to get into an IIT, tolerated engineering classes to get a degree and went on to write the laborious civil service examination. It troubles me when I see IAS aspirants toil for years to get through a tough examination and waste the prime of their youth in not-so-productive rote. Aiyar gives me and my ilk solace and self-esteem.

Nevertheless, the views of Aiyar are natural in the VUCA world we are living in; VUCA stands for Vulnerability, Uncertainty, Complexity and Ambiguity. The nature of truth has become contentious because we are part of a fast-changing complex system. Perceptions of reality today are poles apart, primarily because we do not completely understand the complexities and ambiguities of our fast-changing world and different people base their views on different parameters.

This book attempts to be a primer to make sense of the digital economy and how it has changed our times. The truth of tech stocks lies on a continuum – great companies of the future are at one end and unsustainable businesses are at the other end. Someone who can understand this continuum can make a fortune. Until now, I have taken a maximalist position with respect to the digital economy. It is important to temper this maximalist position with caution, and there are many factors that an investor in the digital economy should be cautious about. Ambiguity in valuations, risk of disruption and regulatory backlash are a few of the threats that can affect the entire digital economy.

The Hard to Value Stuff

Once upon a time, there was a great leader in a South Indian state. As the urban legend goes, the great leader had a great vision for transforming the state's capital into a hub of industries. Destiny smiled upon him and made him a minister so he could lead his people on the path of his great vision. His vision was simple – the government would provide prime land around the state capital at cheap rates to industrialists, MNCs and rich entrepreneurs, with a condition that they would use the land for building industries. When industries came to the capital city, there would be more economic activity and more locals will get jobs. When large MNCs came, many ancillaries would develop around them. Over time, industrial clusters would form. Clusters are associated with lower production cost, which in turn attract more businesses to set up their factories in the cluster.

And he did just that. But while at it, he decided to take something for himself on the side. So any company which got prime land at a nominal price had to pay a kickback that ranged between 40 to 60 per cent of the market price of that land. The kickback ran into thousands of crore. It would be a challenge for corporate houses to generate that much cash to pay, and it would be challenging for the minister to receive and store such huge amounts in cash. His financial advisers came up with a solution to the problem – the bribe-payers would subscribe to shares of shell companies at high valuations. Such shell companies would be under the minister's control. For example, a shell company with 1,000 shares each with a face value of ₹10 would offer 100 shares to bribe-payers at a value of ₹1 crore per share. These 100 shares would fetch ₹100 crore to the shell company. The rest of the 900 shares would be owned by benamidars (name lenders) or proxies of the minister. Thus the minister would control 90 per cent of the voting power in the shell company that had a bank balance of ₹100 crore.

The minister found this to be a convenient way of receiving bribes. No headache of moving cash, no concerns about getting apprehended by tax officials and the security of a bank to keep the ill-gotten wealth safely. Over time, it is said, the minister came to own many shell companies with fat bank balances and transferred ownership of some of these companies from benamidars to his son. After all, he had to pass on his legacy to his son – the leader his people deserved.

As every fairy tale comes to an end, so did the minister's. Quite tragically, he was crossing a river with bundles of cash when his boat capsised and he fell into crocodile-infested waters. He tried to bribe the crocodiles with the bundles of cash, but somehow they did not understand the value of money and made a fine dinner of him.

After his tragic death, competitors within his party tried to sideline his son. But they could not do that because of the immense resources at his disposal. Piqued at the wealth the son enjoyed, the story goes, his political rivals complained to central agencies. The agencies swooped in and soon figured out the modus operandi. They were not pleased that the tax consultants had been able to pull off such a smart move.

It is speculated that this story (whether true or a myth) triggered a new provision in the Income Tax Act to tax any investment in a privately held company of an amount above the fair market value of its shares. This provision – Section 56(2)(viib) of the Income Tax Act – later became infamous as the 'angel tax'.

I tried hard to find the veracity of the story behind angel tax, but could not get any real leads. This story is a myth of sorts, narrated in mirth by advocates and tax professionals, but the modus operandi was real. Such modus operandi of laundering bribe money was unearthed in many investigations. For example, in the case of Y.S. Jagan Mohan Reddy, the CBI alleged (based on evidence recovered in income tax raids) that he had assets disproportionate to his known sources of income. In this case, the Supreme Court recorded in 2013:

> ... son of Late Dr. Y.S. Rajasekhara Reddy, the then Chief Minister of Andhra Pradesh, has adopted several ingenious ways to amass illegal wealth which resulted in great public injury. The then Chief Minister of the State abused his public office to the benefit of his son Y.S. Jagan Mohan Reddy (A-1). Since May, 2004, A-1 started floating a number of companies including M/s Jagathi Publications Pvt. Ltd., which was originally incorporated as a private limited company on 14.11.2006 and later converted into a public limited company on 12.01.2009. At the relevant time, Y.S. Jagan Mohan Reddy (A-1) was designated as the Authorised Signatory to operate the Bank accounts of the said Company. He was appointed as a Director and Chairman with effect

> from 21.06.2007. It is alleged that A-1 floated M/s Jagathi Publications Pvt. Ltd. with an objective of conducting media business with the ill-gotten wealth. Most of the shareholders were alleged to be the benamis of Y.S. Jagan Mohan Reddy (A-1). Further, as a quid pro quo to these investments, the benefits were received by various investors including the companies/individuals from the decisions of the State Government in allotment of lands for Special Economic Zones (SEZs), contracts for irrigation projects, special relaxations/permissions for real estate ventures, mines etc. It is further revealed that Y.S. Jagan Mohan Reddy (A-1) laundered the bribe money by routing it through various individuals and companies and getting investments made by them in his companies at a high premium.[4]

The allegation against Jagan Mohan Reddy was that he laundered bribe money by routing the money through benamidars and getting investments from bribe givers in his companies at a price much higher than the fair market value of his companies.

Section 56(2)(viib) sought to tax the differential amount of investment (i.e., the purchase price minus the fair market value) in an unlisted company as income. It was an anti-abuse measure with the intent to tax bribes that were laundered so blatantly. But the provision had unintended consequences. Start-ups also do what shell companies do. They raise funding at obscenely high valuations. While shell companies have no activity in their books, start-ups are often in the red and their book value is often negative. Tax men (and women) started questioning the high premiums paid by investors for companies that had negative net worth. Consequently, investment from genuine angel investors in start-ups got taxed under this provision. This is the reason why this provision is often called angel tax.

It was not that start-ups lacked documentation to justify their high valuation. They provided discounted cash flow (DCF) charts to justify the high valuations. But the tragedy of DCF is that it can be used to arrive at any figure the valuer wants!

Broadly, there are three approaches to value a company – cost approach, market approach and income approach.

Cost approach tries to develop a value based on real accounting costs. The book value is a valuation under the cost approach. It merely subtracts the company's liabilities from assets to find the company's net worth and treats net worth as the company's value. This method fails miserably for start-ups because they have losses in their start-up phase and have a negative net worth.

Market approach values a start-up by comparing it with similarly placed listed companies. A typical valuation methodology under this approach tries to find the price-to-earnings ratio (P/E) of similar companies that are listed and apply this ratio to the start-up being valued.

Using this approach for start-ups has two sets of challenges. First, it is difficult to find similar companies that are listed, because start-ups work on novel ideas or technology. Second, start-ups do not have any earnings, and therefore the P/E ratio cannot be used as a metric. Valuers have adapted to the first challenge by taking broadly comparable companies to benchmark the start-up. They have coped with the second challenge by substituting P/E with price-to-sales ratio. So if a broadly comparable company listed on the stock market has a market capitalisation of ten times its sales (i.e., 10X), then the start-up would also be valued at 10X of its sales. This improvised method is devoid of all conceptual underpinnings of the market approach, but it works because it is simple and easy to understand. A sales multiple as fair market value is better than another method that does not work.

This simplistic valuation also creates perverse incentives in certain start-ups as it shifts entrepreneurs' focus from profits to sales and some companies readily book losses in order to expand sales and increase valuation.

The income approach states that the value of a company is its ability to generate free cash flows in the future. This is conceptually the strongest but practically the hardest to determine measure of value. The most preferred method under the income approach, the DCF, requires the valuer to forecast the income the company would generate in all future years and discount them to find the present value. Projections of future cash flows can be as conservative or as delusory as the valuer wants. DCF still works decently for a factory establishment since the average capacity utilisation and market demand for the product can be reasonably estimated. But for start-ups, the possibilities are immense. A start-up's core asset is an idea that it seeks to implement using technical knowhow or intellectual property. How can you forecast future income from the initial execution of an idea?

Every time I write a book, I am sure that it is destined to be a bestseller. I often discount my future royalty income and discover a figure that makes me feel like a billionaire. But somehow, the readers in this country are not mature enough to appreciate a great book and I end up with just enough royalty to pay for a single day's lunch.

No wonder the DCF remains the most reliable and also the most unreliable method of valuation at the same time. You can guess what happens when regulators start using it to determine your tax liability. Litigation mounts up, because if no two people can agree to a valuation, there is no way your assessing officer is going to agree with you. This is what happened with the angel tax. But recognising how angel tax adversely affected start-ups, policymakers took many proactive steps to mitigate the litigation risk.

What is true in the start-up stage for a platform company is also true in the post start-up stage. In interviews with bankers and investors, I often ask them if they have a trick to find a good approximation of the value of platform companies. The reply is always in the negative.

Anand Dutta, my batch mate from IIT Kharagpur and now an investor with Nexus Venture Partners, has an interesting take on investing in platform companies. Dutta believes that the platform business model has immense potential to ease life and create value, so much so that he left an established and well-paying job to join a platform start-up at a much lower salary. Today he is a PE investor and is on the board of many new-age tech firms. In spite of his belief in power of platforms, he suggests that value investors should be careful while putting money in new-age tech platforms. They are nascent business models and it is not easy to understand them and appreciate their associated risks! Dutta reminds me that the famous value investor Warren Buffet does not dabble in stocks of platform companies, sticking to his very famous advice of investing only in businesses you deeply understand. Dutta believes that a retail investor with a risk appetite and long-term view should buy into listed platform companies but preferably 3–4 quarters after the IPO; a price discovery happens by then, since some of these companies are good bets in the long term only at the right prices.

When I interviewed a former investment banker, now the chief finance officer (CFO) of a Bengaluru-based software company, his warning was even more ominous. He said that the volume of trading in the Indian market was not high. Most listed stocks, other than the ones with large market capitalisation, do not have a high volume of trading. Price discovery does not happen when the volume of transactions is low. He had some other peeves against tech stocks. According to him, many of the platform companies that float IPOs are severely deficient in making full disclosure. For example, they do not give a break-up of their revenues and the different streams from which they have received the revenues. Most of them do not disclose segments, nor do they declare the losses incurred separately in different business segments.

I like to believe that valuation-related ambiguity calls for caution, but not complete renouncement. We learnt in the last two chapters that some platform companies of today will go on to dominate the market for their services in the future. Such dominance in one field will give them immense leverage, which they can use to impose some form of tax or toll. As a result, the profits such companies will generate in the future will definitely be more than what valuers would have predicted – new avenues of earning revenues will emerge when the company will acquire market power. It is possible to identify such platform companies by analysing the strength of their network effects and their network strategy. When people invest in such a company, they effectively acquire a piece of digital infrastructure.

Regulators Are Coming

While globally Google has a market share in the search engine market of over 90 per cent, in China its market share is less than 3 per cent. Google had entered mainland China in 2006 but pulled out in 2010 after it could not cope with the censorship norms of the Chinese establishment, regular interference and a possible hack. About 85 per cent of users in China use Baidu, a local search engine that has the blessings of the Chinese Communist Party and works within the framework of complex regulations set by it.

It is obvious that a business cannot be successful in a country in which laws do not allow it to operate seamlessly. Whenever any innovation is first introduced, there are often no rules to regulate it. Only after a widespread adoption of the innovation, authorities wake up and frame rules to regulate its operation. Successful platform companies have, till date, had the benefit of operating without any kind of regulatory oversight. Governments around the world have started to catch up with them only in mid-2010s. For example, earlier there was no restriction on digital platforms on how they could monetise data. The jurisprudence on user privacy developed only in the 2010s. In 2016, the European Union (EU) introduced the Global Data Protection Regulation (GDPR), a tough privacy law that imposes many onerous obligations on platforms with respect to user data. As of January 2024, many countries are actively debating data nationalisation laws that could restrict the seamless flow of data across national borders and thus limit the scope of monetisation.

China has been a frontrunner in regulating and controlling digital companies. The 'Great Firewall of China' refers to actions by Chinese authorities of heavily censoring and controlling internet traffic across its borders. While China represents an extreme, many countries around the world feel the need to regulate how digital companies operate in their jurisdiction. The response I received on interviewing policy analysts working in this area is that once a digital platform attains a dominant position, it ceases to be just a platform. It becomes a public utility, just like canals, roads and power utilities. Take for example, Google Maps. When there was no Google Maps, we asked around and wandered about a locality to reach a destination. But today Google Maps represents a necessity for every city-based navigator. In a way, Google Maps has become a public good or utility. It is, thus, the responsibility of the government to ensure that the service is delivered seamlessly to people and is not abused in any way.

As regulations are still evolving, I perceive them as a major threat to the rise of digital platforms.

A related issue is the risk of the State competing with platforms to provide the same marketplace. Developing a network in the start-up phase is always costly for platforms, and it makes no sense for a State to waste taxpayer money in developing such a network. But once a network has been established, it is actually pretty easy for the State to poach the network. The State can use both formal and informal means to prop up a state-owned enterprise to seize the network.

But such a strategy on the part of the State will be the exception rather than the rule. State-owned enterprises often cannot operate platforms as efficiently as private entrepreneurs can. Nor are they, by their very nature, agile in adopting new technologies. When would the State be inclined to compete with private entrepreneurs in running a platform? When there is a national security concern or it is imperative as a part of public policy, that is, when the State feels that the services provided by a platform are public utilities and need to be equitably distributed to citizens. A case in point is the Open Network for Digital Commerce (ONDC), a State-backed network in India that seeks to connect buyers and sellers across verticals – electronics, grocery, food delivery, tours and whatnot. One of the stated objectives of ONDC is to 'create a level playing field for e-commerce behemoths such as Amazon, Flipkart, and offline traders who have been crying foul at the unfair trade practices of these e-tailers',[5] that is, to curb digital monopolies.

It is too early to say how effective ONDC will be to democratise e-tail business, or what impact it will have on platform companies. However, we can get clues from the way public and private players are competing in the field of card payments. We had seen in Chapter 3 how Visa and Mastercard run a virtual duopoly in card payments and the market power they wield. They have complained to the United States Trade Representative (USTR) that the Indian government engages in public lobbying to promote RuPay card, which does not allow Visa and Mastercard a level playing field.

The complaint appears baseless because the Indian government would, of course, promote a business run by it (like any other promoter would). The government encourages public sector banks to adopt RuPay, a non-profit venture, just like private companies resort to cross-selling of their products. It promotes RuPay card as a part of its larger agenda to develop a cashless economy and discourage people from transacting in cash (thus there is a public policy angle). The government has also introduced a statutory provision (Section 269SU of the Income Tax Act) that all Indian companies with turnover of more than ₹50 crore should offer RuPay payment options to their customers, or face penalties.

It is noteworthy that RuPay's share of debit and credit cards issued in India has meteorically risen from 15 per cent in 2017 to 63 per cent in November 2020 (thus shrinking the percentage share of rivals Visa and Mastercard).[6] The volume of transactions through Visa and Mastercard is still disproportionately higher, but RuPay card makes sure they don't wield duopoly powers in the Indian market any longer.

Another instance of the State's interest in platform business is an all-encompassing digital public infrastructure called 'India Stack' that intends to supply government-generated data to application developers for developing innovative applications across multiple sectors.[7] Aadhaar, United Payments Interface (UPI) as well as ONDC are a part of India Stack. India Stack will, no doubt, accelerate the pace of innovation and promote competition, but it can be bad news for the entrenched platforms.

Geopolitical factors also increase the regulatory risk for digital platforms. Consider the case of platforms that have thrived on Chinese investments. They are directly affected by geopolitical factors playing out elsewhere.

To take a brief detour, China and the United States are in the midst of a competition to lap up the benefits of the fourth industrial revolution, which is an umbrella term for new technologies that could become general purpose technologies. The fourth industrial revolution relies heavily on digitisation and the 5G network. As a part of its strategy to benefit from the fourth industrial revolution, China is pushing its technological standards in other markets. Naturally India, being a major market as well as an incubator of tech innovation, is important for China. Meanwhile, India is wary of Chinese aggression along its borders and the Line of Actual Control (LAC).

India has multiple concerns about Chinese investment in Indian start-ups, and rightly so. First, China's strategy for global dominance includes a plan to control digital infrastructure and digital platforms in emerging economies, the largest of which happens to be India. Various projects emanating from China to effect this plan are together termed as 'Digital BRI'. While India has refused to be a part of China's Belt and Road Initiative (BRI), you will be surprised to know that Digital BRI's biggest footprint is in India. Between 2012 and 2020, China has invested almost US$6 billion on digital infrastructure in India.

Figure 4.1: China's spending on Digital Silk Road projects, by country

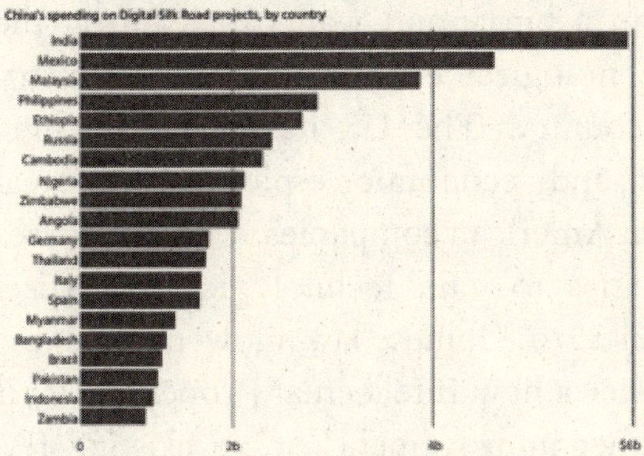

Source: Alex Capri, 2020; reproduced with permission

This does not necessarily imply any designs of the country to colonise India's digital and telecom infrastructure. Alex Capri of the Hinrich Foundation, who also taught me trade policy at the Lee Kuan Yew School of Public Policy, says, 'The establishment of Chinese digital hegemony over a large swathe of the earth could make Chinese standards in 5G, cloud infrastructure, smartphones and other technologies the de facto standard for a large part of the so-called emerging world. The plan, then, is to create a virtuous cycle for both the Chinese state and its champion tech companies, giving them even more scale and greater market advantages.'[8] But effectively, a hegemonic control over India's digital infrastructure can give China leverage over India's digital economy.

Second, the issue is China's techno-nationalism. The weird-sounding term refers to China's national desire to be the most advanced country in the world technologically. It believes that technological dominance is intricately linked to economic and political dominance. And rightly so, just as American hegemony flows from its defence and civil technologies.

But China is in a hurry and wants to leapfrog the evolution of technological expertise that an industry follows in any country. The US has accused China of using cyber and economic espionage to steal technologies from American companies. China also uses subversive strategies to gain technological expertise. For instance, until 2019, Chinese law allowed a Chinese company to register a new Intellectual Property (IP) if it made any 'further improvement' on an existing IP.[9] So Chinese companies borrowed technologies from foreign companies through a licensing agreement and then patented the same technology by making cosmetic improvements. This effectively allowed Chinese firms to overtake the foreign companies they borrowed IPs from.

Chinese techno-nationalism becomes a threat for India because of an entirely different reason. In a 2014 essay called 'Why China Can't Innovate', Harvard Business Review explained that China relies heavily on top-down planning for technological progress. This, in turn, stifles creativity, which is essentially a bottom-up process. To make up for this shortcoming, Chinese firms aggressively acquire start-ups working on promising new technologies. This presents a threat to India's tech clusters in Bengaluru, Gurugram, Hyderabad and so on.

There is a real fear of Chinese firms acquiring a large stake in an Indian firm just to gain access to new technical know-how and overwhelm the Indian company. When this happens, the Indian firm effectively loses its competitive advantage.

Third, Chinese companies having control over platforms run in India may misuse the data collected from Indian users for surveillance on behalf of the Chinese State. This concern arises because of a lack of a clear boundary between the State and private corporations in China.[10]

The first issue discussed above is a leverage India has: of being the largest market in the developing world where the race to leadership over the fourth industrial revolution will play out. This leverage could be used as a measure of economic warfare on the face of an increasingly belligerent Chinese Army at India's borders. The second and third issues are clearly matters of concern for the Indian security establishment. In either case, the risk of regulatory action on start-ups funded by Chinese companies increases manifold.

The politics of data presents many uncertainties for platform companies. The first is the uncertainty surrounding data processing. Many platform companies make profits primarily by monetising user data. In India, this includes (a) Foreign-resident platforms (such as Google, Facebook and Twitter); (b) Indian-resident platforms that have externalised and have migrated their headquarters abroad (such as Practo and GupShup)[11] and (c) Indian-resident platforms. Platforms which have their headquarters abroad generate data from users resident in India. So data generation takes place in India, but this data is stored in an offshore server or cloud service and data processing is done abroad.

Data processing is a necessary step for monetisation – the company gets insights into user behaviour by processing the data. The platform company then shows its income from monetisation in the country in which data processing takes place. In many cases, data processing is done in low-tax jurisdictions due to tax considerations. A narrative that is becoming increasingly loud is that large digital platforms are not paying their fair share of taxes in the country where they generate data. They do not leave any profit in India even though they get all their data from India.

This argument is valid only for platform companies that actually make profits. Most indigenous platform companies are still in the red and making losses. Hence, taxes are not a major consideration for them. But the perception that platform companies do not leave any profit in the host country where data generation takes place has created a demand for data localisation. Data localisation would force a company to process data in the host country itself and all profits from its monetisation would be booked there.

Data privacy norms are often bundled with data localisation policy. Data privacy norms stem from the idea that digital platforms' data management needs to be monitored and regulated lest they misuse user data and breach the privacy of individual data users. Platform companies usually anonymise user data before processing it for generating user insights. However, privacy is too sensitive an issue to be left to self-regulation. Hence, data privacy norms. Stringent data privacy norms can impose significant compliance costs on platform companies and can even dry up a major source of revenue – data monetisation.

Platforms and Economic Development

The story of platforms is not complete without a discussion of their direct role in economic development, especially in developing countries. This is another way of analysing the value of platforms – measure their role in driving economic development in the poorest of countries.

But for that we need to take a detour to understand what drives economic development. It is difficult to give an answer to this question in any size less than a hefty tome. Researchers in development economics have identified myriad factors that catalyse economic development and are still not sure which factors work in which specific conditions to trigger development.

To understand economic development, economists often compare developed countries with developing countries. They use indicators such as the GDP to explain why the rich are rich and the poor are poor. One popular explanation is that people in developed countries are more entrepreneurial and solution-oriented, due to which they drive innovation, due to which productivity increases and businesses prosper, due to which GDPs of such countries are high. This seems to imply that people in developing countries are less entrepreneurial.

This belief that people from developing countries are less entrepreneurial is deeply ingrained in academic literature too. The German sociologist Max Weber had demonstrated in his seminal work *Protestant Ethics and the Spirit of Capitalism* that some cultures are more entrepreneurial than others. In a follow-up book called *The Religion of India: The Sociology of Hinduism and Buddhism*, he claimed that Hindus were underdeveloped and colonised because of a fatalistic attitude. This attitude develops in Hindus because of a belief in reincarnation and preordained fate (what Hindus call karma). Back in 1963, the development economist K. William Kapp traced the source of Indian poverty to fatalism in Hindu culture.[12] So culture leads to fatalism, which leads to risk aversion, which leads to lack of enterprise, which leads to economic stagnation. Many Indian academicians have also supported this causality.

Thankfully, all this is just academic hubris and populations following Hinduism and Buddhism are not doomed. The economist Ha-Joon Chang tears into the logic that people in developed countries are more entrepreneurial by simply comparing the challenges faced by people from developing countries.[13] An entrepreneur in a developed country faces only a fraction of the challenges an entrepreneur in a developing country faces. Doing business in a developing country is not easy – the entrepreneur has to manage unpredictable logistics, difficult credit situations, non-existent infrastructure and much more. In comparison, entrepreneurs in developed countries have much fewer unpredictable factors to navigate. They work in sanitised and predictable business ecosystems and have easy access to capital and resources. So people in developing countries, who have grown up with field-training in making the most of scarce resources, are more entrepreneurial than people in developed countries.

Then, what is the secret behind the wealth of developed countries? Chang says that what matters for economic development is not entrepreneurship but how entrepreneurship is organised. Stated simply, if individual entrepreneurship can be organised well, the economic output is more than the output from the sum of individual entrepreneurship.

There is no one-size-fits-all formula for how countries can organise entrepreneurship. Western European countries managed this in the aftermath of the Second World War by strengthening private firms. They used the ideology of capitalism to justify this approach of putting their weight behind private firms. In Japan, social conformity is high, which makes it easy to organise individual entrepreneurship into strong firms. Japan received independence from the United States in 1952 and turned into the biggest economic challenger of the United States in the 1970s. South Korea transformed from an underdeveloped country to a highly developed country in a matter of two decades, a success story that is often referred to as the 'Miracle on the Han River'. South Korea had an entirely different approach – its development came under a dictator by the name of General Park Chung Hee. General Park used authoritarianism to enforce conformity and backed a handful of chaebols (family-run firms) as agents of economic growth. China, on the other hand, relied on a variety of tools and relied heavily on State-owned entities to organise individual entrepreneurship.

So there is no one way of organising entrepreneurship to initiate growth, but the organisation of entrepreneurship is more important than the individual entrepreneur. This inference is not a new one. After all, civilisation developed when chieftains and kings organised people to develop cities. Giza's famous pyramids could not have been constructed some 2,500 years before the current era without organisation. However, this inference is an important one, because the role of organisation in economic growth is often undervalued by economists.

Successful countries place a lot of emphasis on cooperation and collaboration. Countries of Western Europe, which fought many wars among themselves for about a millennium till the end of the Second World War, took to cooperation and collaboration so well thereafter that they managed to politically integrate and form the European Union and European Economic Area, the largest common market in the world.

There is nothing great about collaboration, one could say. If collaboration is the trick, then why can't the least developed countries prosper? Consider a typical village in a developing country like India. When you go to the village, you would be amazed to see their warmth and hospitality. All villagers seem to know each other; they are always ready to help you when you forget your way around the village market. All villagers dress alike, behave alike. But the closer you look, the deeper are the divisions you see. The villagers are divided on the basis of religion, caste, creed and social status. An informal hierarchy exists in the village between people belonging to different groups. Discrimination against some groups is clear from social interactions. Dominant groups have had their fights, which the village historians would eagerly narrate over a long drag of hookah. Persons of some minority groups who stay in the same locality are ever fearful of inter-group conflict. You end up realising that the biggest *unit of collaboration* is the kin group. If the village is located in a patriarchal society, the biggest *unit of cooperation* is the kin group minus women of the family, because, they say, women are the family's honour and have to be protected by being kept under lock and key.

You also observe that collaboration does happen across groups. Groups collaborate for the annual village fair, for a marriage in the village and also during the harvesting season. But such collaboration is mediated by continuous negotiations and bargaining. A natural leader does not emerge from the group interactions, because a leader from X faith, Y tribe and Z kinship is an XYZ and is not acceptable to someone who is not X or not Y or not Z. Any collaborative project is mired by continuous politics and negotiations for allocation of resources. The social hierarchy of groups plays a role in sustaining distrust among them. Because there is no community, people do not understand the concept of 'common goods' which are for the welfare of the community. Any man who is in a position of power (say the village chief) is expected by his group to siphon off common goods for himself and his group (women are expected to follow the diktats of their husbands). When a person with a high sense of morality does not misuse their position to help themselves to public resources, they are ridiculed behind the back for being naive and slow-witted.

Ideally, hierarchy should help in easier collaboration. We have seen many countries with hierarchical social orders prosper and develop. But the problem in developing countries is that the social hierarchy does not have any legitimacy. Some groups claim superiority because of their place in the traditional class or caste pyramid. Others claim superiority based on their wealth. Still other groups claim superiority because of their numerical strength, which can be used to win any brawl. Those lower in the hierarchy have their own narratives about why and how they have been historically wronged. In short, it is not a clear hierarchy, nor is it a legitimate one. A tentative hierarchy only serves to confuse every person's social interactions and increases the unpredictability of inter-group interactions.

What is true for a typical village is true for organisations in towns as well. Firms have their internal divisions, which can be much more complex than those in villages. Factories have clear class divisions; the owner's relatives form one class, managers form a second class and workers form a third class. Every person is reminded of their class inside the factory. Workers cannot sit side-by-side with managers, cannot call them by name. Persons of different classes have different canteen facilities and differential access to common work resources. Sociologists have found that higher castes (or dominant tribes, as the case may be) have a disproportionately high representation in manager class, while lower castes (or minority ethnic groups) have a higher representation in worker class. Plus, the promoters generally belong to merchant communities. In such a situation, workers may not feel a sense of belonging or responsibility for the firm. Internal office politics among managers, and between managers and the promoter group, can be intense and consume productive time. Labour unrest and absenteeism will naturally be high in these situations.

What happens in private firms also repeats in government departments, although in a different form. Due to reservation in government jobs for weaker sections, they have significant representation in government offices. But government offices are traditionally obsessed with hierarchy. Employees are divided into groups, quite literally. Group A are senior officers, Group B are junior officials, Group C are clerical staff and Group D are peons. When a Group A officer presses a bell, a Group C staff comes running to take notes or a Group D to serve tea. Officials of different groups are allotted different residential quarters.

There is a good chance that Group C and Group D officials do not feel a sense of pride or belonging towards the organisation or the work they do. They do not see themselves as a part of a larger governance project.

Even within Group A, the hierarchy can be treacherous. Group A may be subdivided into services. The military services or intelligence services or administrative services may be at the top of an internal hierarchy of services. To keep reminding other services of their place in the hierarchy, the dominant service would have their officers in all the top posts and make senior officers of an inferior service report to junior officers of the dominant service. In a developed country, no one would take offence in reporting to a much younger person, if merited. But where hierarchy is ubiquitous, officers take offence in reporting to a junior. This results in hilarious turf wars, competition for resources and continuous conflict in the workplace. There is wasteful competition between agencies and departments working at cross purpose, branches hiding information from each other and insecure ministries working to curb the power of their own agencies.

Further, since there are so many divisions in the community, individual government servants don't necessarily sympathise with government projects that are meant for the common public good and so may not hesitate to divert government resources for personal gain.

So collaboration is not as simple as it seems. Developed countries have systematically erased ethnic boundaries (and have been largely successful), while developing countries are still coping with these challenge. These boundaries are ancient, and it is not politically easy to remove them. Some developing countries try to find a middle path, a unity in diversity, but unity in the real sense is practically difficult to achieve as long as diversity is arranged hierarchically.

Sometimes, different countries see these sociological constructs differently. To cite a simple anecdote from sociology textbooks, the word 'secularism' has different meanings in a typical European country and in a typical developing country. In a European country, secularism means complete divorce between religious organisations and the State. But in a typical developing country, secularism means equal treatment of all religions in the State's dealings with religion. European countries enforce a single unified code of law as part of their notion of secularism, thus reducing differences in legal practices between communities. But in developing countries, secularism involves equal respect and tolerance for personal laws of religious groups. This reinforces differences between communities.

Ethnic divisions come naturally. But movement from ethnic identity to global identity is not natural. Societies progress from diverse identities to unity-in-diversity to national and global identities. This progress is slow and not automatic. For this progress to happen, a leader acceptable to a majority has to emerge and clamp down on elites of ethnic groups. School education and narratives play a major role in strengthening national or global identities. A little bit of authoritarianism helps speed up the process. But an authoritarian may turn out to be a crony capitalist like Saddam Hussein and not a visionary like Park Chung Hee. There are just too many variables in this social engineering process, which is why countries in Africa and the Middle East are unable to erase ethnic boundaries and are thus unable to harness the economic benefits of cooperation and collaboration.

Coming back to platforms, what do they do best? Platforms are a new model of organising the actions of users. A platform can be called a multi-sided market, but it is ultimately an administrative system that manages and organises the action of users on different sides. The users don't have to know each other. Even when they know each other, their interaction is based on their digital identity which hides their social identity. Platforms excel in organising individual entrepreneurship of millions of users and deriving synergy benefits from such organisation. They amplify the process of cooperation and collaboration between users irrespective of their social background.

Platforms can be a game-changer for developing countries. Already, municipal administrations in major Indian cities are creating platforms to provide civic amenities more efficiently – smart parking solutions (a list of all public and private parking facilities, made available on mobile apps), emergency response through mobile apps, smart public transport solutions (real-time tracking of bus movements), incident alert apps, apps for accessing and monitoring public goods and so on. These are all new strategies for organising activities at the grassroot level. The proactive adoption of platforms by governments has led to the delivery of better services, transparently and without discrimination.

In the private sector, platforms have demonstrated how well they can organise entrepreneurial activities. While Amazon states that it provides a marketplace for entrepreneurs and consumers to meet, it is actually doing much more. Its interaction with suppliers is wider than just providing them access to the Amazon app. It provides sellers with several options for storage, packaging and delivery. It tracks customer orders, sales growth and does payment settlements for sellers. Instead of managing their own storage, packaging and customer analytics, entrepreneurs can now concentrate on what they do best – product development. Amazon brings in its own economies of scale and automation processes, thus reducing costs and improving productivity at the same time. What Amazon does could have been done by entrepreneurs through merchant associations, if they managed to organise themselves. But it is difficult to organise individual entrepreneurs on scale and provide them a strong institutional framework, especially in developing countries where power and politics mire merchant associations.

Platforms can play an important role in economic development because they present innovative solutions for organising entrepreneurship. As more firms in developing countries adopt a platform strategy to organise business, they will be unlocking value and growing productivity exponentially. For investors, this can be a new approach to assess the value of platform companies and also companies that are adopting platform strategies. The question they need to ask is – which companies are using a platform strategy to solve the problem of organisation? Which companies are using a platform strategy to organise individual entrepreneurship? Which companies are using platforms to organise their employees and customers in a better way?

For policymakers, platform strategy presents a new opportunity to circumvent the challenges of strong ethnic identities. Platforms do not solve all problems arising from ethnic differences among citizens, but they solve many. They provide developing countries an opportunity to leap-frog to a new stage of economic development without having to perform the social engineering required to suppress ethnic identities and strengthen national identity among citizens.

Conclusion

On balance, the key vulnerability of platform companies is that they have a binary future – they will either crush competition and dominate, or perish. In that sense, investing in platform companies can be considered a risky investment. However, an understanding of networks and how they work can help a lay person differentiate between competitors in an emerging field and identify those few which have a potential to succeed.

Digital technology is evolving at an exponential pace and the curve is far from plateauing. New technologies help in developing new factors of value creation, which means wealth creation for those who own the new factors. Passive investors miss out on this wealth creation because they fear what they do not understand. Some other passive investors put their eggs in the wrong baskets – because they do not know how the new business models work. My attempt in this chapter, and also in the previous two chapters, was to explain how network effects work – so that even passive investors can correctly assess an investment opportunity that comes their way.

This chapter concludes with a discussion linking platforms to economic development in countries at lower levels of development. The ability of digital platforms to facilitate cooperation and collaboration across wide populations can help in the development process. And thus, in the markets of developing countries, the utility of a platform in organising individual entrepreneurship of masses can be a key factor in assessing its value.

5

Crypto Evangelism

Some folk tales find mention in multiple ancient sources. There is one such folk tale on greed whose plotline can be found in the Jataka tales, Arabian Nights, *The Canterbury Tales* and many other ancient sources. The story goes that once upon a time three robbers happen to chance upon a huge treasure deep inside the woods. They cannot move the treasure since it is dark. So they send the youngest robber to the city to get food and wine. The two guarding the treasure deliberate and decide that they don't have to share the treasure with the third robber if they kill him. The third robber has a similar idea and so laces food and wine with poison before going back into the woods. The first two robbers pounce upon the third robber when he arrives and kill him. Then they eat the poisoned food and wine and meet their death.

Gujarat's Crime Investigation Department (CID) discovered a similar plotline when they investigated a complaint filed by a builder in 2018. The builder, Shailesh Bhatt, had alleged that policemen had extorted Bitcoins worth ₹9 crore from him. When the CID dug deeper, it unearthed an incredible plot involving a series of scams, the victim being the swindler of the previous scam. James Hadley Chase would have loved this hustle.

The story begins on the evening of 8 November 2016, when Prime Minister Narendra Modi declared demonetisation. Before this fateful night, many unknown individuals had diligently engaged in tax evasion and bribery and had stashed away the black money they generated from these activities. This is Swindle No. 1, whose victim was the nation. After demonetisation, an opportunity was provided by the government to use old currency notes till 31 December 2016. In this period, many touts and entrepreneurs ran the business of converting black money in old currency into white money or new currency for a commission. One visionary from Surat by the name of Satish Kumbhani started the Bit Connect Investment Company, which allowed the victims of demonetisation to invest their black money and receive attractive returns. It was a double bonanza: escape the calamity of demonetisation and get market-beating returns. Kumbhani's idea was to launder black money through Bitcoins and make windfall profits from Bitcoin trading. He also floated a new coin by the name of BitConnect and sold it to investors. Over time, Kumbhani stretched his network far and wide, offering irresistible rates of return on investments. His network extended from the United States in the west to South Korea in the east, with Surat as the headquarters.

But as it later transpired, Kumbhani's BitConnect was just another scam that showed get-rich-quick dreams to fleece investors. This was Swindle No. 2. Kumbhani had promised returns that were unsustainable, and the scheme collapsed in January 2018. As per one estimate, its collapse wiped away investments to the tune of USD 2.4 billion.[1] BitConnect's agents in Surat and elsewhere shuttered their shop and went into hiding. In India, BitConnect's agents drew comfort from the fact that most investors had invested their black money and so would not go to the police.

But one of the investors who had lost money took matters into his own hands. Shailesh Bhatt had invested ₹2 crore in BitConnect and could not accept the fact that he was conned. He researched BitConnect, hatched a plan and put together a team. Now, he might be a sharp one, but he did not know how cryptocurrencies like Bitcoin worked. So he included one techie by the name of Kirit Paladiya in his team. Disguising themselves as income tax officials, they raided Piyush Savalia, a BitConnect employee, on 30 January 2018.[2] They took Savalia to a farmhouse and interrogated him about the money taken by BitConnect from investors. Savalia himself was not in possession of any money, but he probably gave them leads. On 1 February, the team kidnapped Dhaval Mavani, a key person associated with BitConnect, and forced him to transfer 2,256 Bitcoins – then worth ₹131 crore – to Bhatt. This was Swindle No. 3 (although it was more of a robbery than swindle). With this, the prey had become the predator – a victim of BitConnect scam had become the perpetrator in the next act.

Then, Kirit Paladiya, the techie who was a part of Bhatt's team, became greedy. He was not happy with the small share of the loot he had received. So he hatched his own plan. While Bhatt had enrolled fake income tax officers for his con, Paladiya inducted real policemen through a middleman to steal Bitcoins from Bhatt.[3] He assured the policemen that Bhatt would not file a complaint because these were Bitcoins Bhatt had stolen.

The policemen kidnapped Bhatt and Paladiya and threatened them of dire consequences if Bhatt did not transfer the Bitcoins to them. Paladiya, who was handling Bhatt's wallet, acted as if he was transferring the Bitcoins to the policemen's wallet. He did not actually transfer the Bitcoins at this time, but made Bhatt believe that he was doing so. Later, when Bhatt and Paladiya were released, Paladiya gave some Bitcoins to the middleman and the police and pocketed the rest. As per the police, he kept 70 per cent of the Bitcoins they swindled from Bhatt. This was Swindle No. 4.

But as it happens in James Hadley Chase novels, Paladiya had misjudged Bhatt. The rational action on part of Bhatt would have been to keep quiet, since he himself had got the money by extortion and kidnapping. But Bhatt was enraged with the police and complained to the state home ministry, which then forwarded the complaint to CID. As CID went about investigating the chain of scams, Bhatt even tried to hide his criminal deeds by offering a bribe to Savalia (the one he had kidnapped) to give a wrong statement to CID!

Kumbhani and Others

Coming back to Satish Kumbhani, the scamster-entrepreneur from Surat was investigated by the Federal Bureau of Investigation (FBI). He received a prison sentence of 38 months in September 2022. However, he has been absconding and his whereabouts are unknown. Sadly, even the FBI could not find him.

The Kumbhani scam is an important study for anyone interested in understanding (or investing in) cryptocurrencies, because it clearly illustrates which cryptos could be an investment fraud and which are not. Kumbhani developed a digital token called the BitConnect Coin or BCC sometime in 2016. Kumbhani claimed on the BitConnect website that BCC 'is an open source, peer-to-peer, community driven decentralized cryptocurrency' and that it was based on 'decentralized blockchain transaction technology, so no centralized third party to trust [sic]. Transactions are performed directly between the users.'[4] This was a blatantly false statement, for BCC was *not* decentralised. Kumbhani exercised central control over the blockchain. And this is where, as we shall later discuss, lies the key difference between investment fraud and a trustless system.

Kumbhani floated an Initial Coin Offering (ICO) between November 2016 and January 2017 (i.e., during demonetisation). He offered BCC for Bitcoins. His business model involved selling BCC for an assured return that went up to 40 per cent per month.[5] Investors bought BCCs by paying Bitcoins and were assured that they would get back the investment with high returns whenever they decided to encash the BCCs. It was basically a Ponzi scheme.

BCC spread swiftly. By January 2018, when it went bust, it had a large number of investors in ninety-five countries.[6] This was largely possible because BCC had appointed agents in all these countries. Agents were recruited from existing investors and were paid handsome referral commissions. A multilevel marketing structure was used to earn commissions. In a multilevel marketing model, the individual, say A, who gets a new investor B receives a percentage of the new investment as commission. The investor B, who then gets C to the scheme, gets a percentage of the new investment as commission. The individual A who had referred B to the scheme also gets a share of the new investment from C as commission. Similarly, when C gets investor D, all of A, B and C get a commission from D's investment. And so on and so forth.

In this manner, Kumbhani was running a typical Ponzi scheme. In the garb of running a peer-to-peer, community driven decentralised cryptocurrency, he was raising money from the public. To entice investors, he promised unrealistic returns that BitConnect could not possibly earn through honest means. BitConnect also paid about 13 per cent of new investments as referral commission.[7] Since it could not make enough profits to pay 13 per cent commission and 40 per cent return on investment per month, BitConnect basically paid the older investors from new investments.

In my book *The Great Indian Fraud*, I have discussed the case of Amit Bhardwaj (the Bitcoin Ponzi King) who used a very similar modus operandi to defraud investors of Bitcoins worth more than ₹500 crore. Many such cases of fraud have been detected in the crypto space. This allows many to generalise all cryptocurrencies as fraudulent.

The truth remains that the blockchain technology is revolutionary and will change the world in unpredictable ways. Cryptocurrencies are going to change the nature of money. There is significant value in the blockchain technology as well as in the virtual currencies based on this technology.

History is evidence to the fact that genuine innovation breeds fraudsters. In the 1700s, advances in British navigation opened up the prospects of high profits from richly endowed colonies in the New World, and this led to the South Sea Bubble that burst in 1720. In the 1840s, advances in rail technology led to reduced travel times, leading to an investment frenzy. The internet technology held new promises in the 1990s,[8] that eventually led to the dotcom crisis discussed in Chapter 2. Quite predictably, fraudsters are using virtual assets as a means to fleece uninformed investors.

The first task in identifying the right cryptocurrency is to separate wheat from the chaff[9]. This chapter primarily identifies different kinds of cryptocurrencies and differentiates them based on their utility as well as their vulnerability to fraud.

Finding the Balance in Virtual Assets

Views on cryptocurrencies are sharply divided. The only other area these days in which views are so polarised is politics, between the rightists and the liberals. Some people argue that cryptocurrencies do not have any underlying or inherent value so they are purely speculative instruments. These naysayers equate crypto mania with tulip mania, an asset bubble of the 17th century in which contract prices for tulip bulbs reached extraordinarily high levels. On the other side are crypto maximalists, who see cryptocurrencies as the future of money.

Interestingly, a large proportion of the elderly are crypto naysayers while a large proportion of young geeks and techies are crypto maximalists. Here is an anecdote to explain the divide. In *The Great Indian Fraud*, I had floated a theory that Bitcoin could be a Ponzi scheme, making its founder – the elusive Satoshi Nakamoto[10] – the greatest swindler the world has ever seen. I had emphasised that it was just a theory, but that did not stop my readers from branding me as a naysayer. One reader took to Twitter, now called 'X' (Figure 5.1), to say that the portion of the book on cryptos seemed 'a little biased' and that was because the author was probably aged!

Figure 5.1: The Tweet

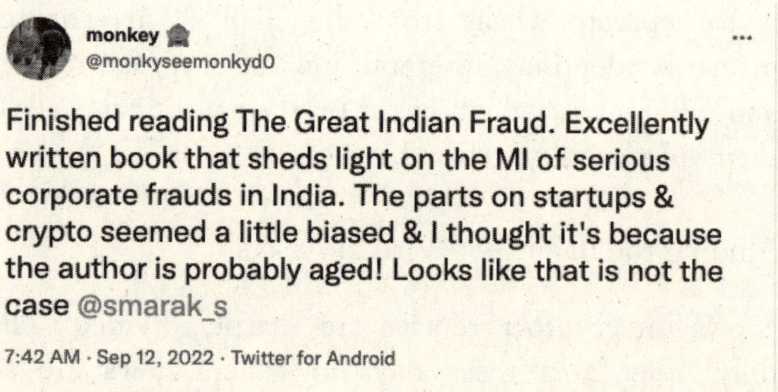

monkey
@monkyseemonkyd0

Finished reading The Great Indian Fraud. Excellently written book that sheds light on the MI of serious corporate frauds in India. The parts on startups & crypto seemed a little biased & I thought it's because the author is probably aged! Looks like that is not the case @smarak_s

7:42 AM · Sep 12, 2022 · Twitter for Android

The divide between naysayers and maximalists arises largely out of an inter-generational divide in understanding the potential of the blockchain technology and cryptocurrencies. Blockchain technology is one of the most potent forces that will drive the Industrial Revolution 4.0. The adoption of this technology will lead to significant value creation. In line with this view, they believe that cryptocurrencies driven by the blockchain technology will revolutionise and democratise money. Naysayers are concerned that this new money has no inherent value and no backing of a sovereign government. Such money can be easily misused.

The naysayers are not wrong in their place. When they find many tokens being misused by fraudsters, or when they see valuations of a new token bouncing off floors and roofs in quick succession, they turn sceptic about cryptocurrencies. There are many instances in which fraudsters and speculators have piggybacked on the cryptocurrency mania to deceive investors. ICOs have been used to raise money from investors with a promise – implicit or explicit – of huge growth in value. Commenting on the rush in the US in 2017 to invest in ICOs, Jeff John Roberts mentions in his book *Kings of Crypto*:

> Never in history has there been an easier way to raise more money from more people with such little effort. The number and size of the ICOs defied logic. Staggering sums changed hands every day. A company called Filecoin, which promised to build a blockchain storage network, raised $205 million. An outfit called Bancor, which touted an online supercurrency, raised $153 million worth of Ethereum in just three hours, while one called Brave – a new web browser – raised $35 million in thirty *seconds*.[11]

There is Bitcoin. And then there are shitcoins. Shitcoins are tokens 'spun up on shaky technology and then flogged in fly-by-night marketing schemes.'[12] Hence, the need to differentiate between different kinds of tokens and understand each one's value proposition.

In this chapter I have introduced cryptocurrencies and differentiated the many types of virtual products being termed as cryptocurrencies. Many of these do not even use cryptography and so are technically not cryptocurrencies. Hence, I will use the wider phrase 'virtual assets' in the rest of the chapter.

The world of virtual assets is new but is rapidly evolving. The underlying technology is novel and dense for the uninitiated. Since a vast majority of people are unfamiliar with virtual assets, most books on the subject (and there are many) start by explaining blockchains, decentralised networks, cryptography, distributed ledger, mining, hardfork, airlift, fungible token, non-fungible token and so on. In this book I have adopted a somewhat contrasting approach. I have left the technical part to the geeks and analysed the value creation that different kinds of virtual assets promise. After all, the excitement in any new tech product is in the value creation that it promises. At times, I will resort to oversimplification in this chapter for the purpose of comprehension.

What Problem Does Cryptocurrency Solve?

As a child, I would greedily devour stories of treasure hunts. A race to reach the pirates' gold safely secreted in an exotic island, rare artefacts hidden in a Pharaoh's tomb, snake-infested forests concealing a mythical city and many more of such stories kept me enthralled. I dreamed of being a treasure hunter when I grew up. And my first job in the IRS was that of a tax sleuth. A key part of a tax sleuth's job is to search for hidden wealth. I have found and seized hordes of cash, precious jewellery and benami assets of tax dodgers. I have found gold in hidden chambers inside washrooms, in wheat sacks inside kitchens, in secret cabinets of customised cars and even inside snake-infested forests. My colleagues were once a part of an income tax raid on an island off the Mumbai coast, but I missed that adventure. Maybe I am living my childhood dream.

Hiding wealth from the tax authorities is a challenge the rich have faced for ages. But the tax collector is not the only predator on the prowl to take your wealth. Smooth-talking but usurious moneylenders, banks, robbers – all are out to grab your wealth.

The rich have faced this problem of hiding their wealth securely because of an inherent constraint of gold (and money) – you cannot have clear *ownership rights* and *anonymity* at the same time. To keep your money secure, you can deposit it in a bank. The money is kept in your name and you have a legal claim over it. Your ownership rights are clear. But your ownership also becomes known to all. The tax officers will come to take their pound of flesh in the form of income tax, wealth tax and inheritance tax. Your ex-wife or relatives may lay claim over it. Your creditors can come for it.

Alternatively, you can dig a pit in your garden and hide the gold or cash. Your wealth remains anonymous, but you have no ownership rights. There is always a risk of losing the money to thieves. Anyone can dig the pit and take the wealth away. This is a problem with benami properties as well. Some people hide their black money by buying properties in the name of a friend or a relative or even an employee – a practice often referred to as benami ownership. The person lending their name may double-cross you, and you can lose your entire wealth.

I have heard stories of many people losing their wealth because they were defrauded by their benamidars.

This is a perplexing dichotomy for the rich – anonymity versus safety. If they hide their wealth from the authorities, they may lose it. If they keep their wealth securely, they can't hide it. Historically, no money has managed to circumvent this dichotomy. You can either have clear ownership rights or anonymity.

Many offshore finance centres (or the 'tax havens') were created to resolve this problem. Tax havens are safe grounds for not only tax-evaded money but also for illegitimately earned money like drug money or blood money. These havens have secrecy laws that prohibit their banks from disclosing client information to anyone. You may deposit your money in a bank in such a jurisdiction and have ownership rights, yet maintain anonymity at the same time. But hoarding money in a tax haven comes with its own set of challenges. One, tax havens are not all that secretive and opaque any more. They have been forced to share information with other countries – on request as well as automatically – in some high-risk situations. Two, the money you maintain in a tax haven cannot be anonymously moved around. Three, the process of bringing the money back home is cumbersome.

So the problem continued to persist, and no store of value managed to resolve this dichotomy. Before Bitcoin.

Attempts to resolve this problem through use of digital technology were made as early as the 1980s. David Lee Chaum, an American computer scientist and cryptographer, invented Digital Cash (DigiCash) in 1983. It was claimed that Digital Cash could be transferred from one person to another anonymously and safely. However, neither DigiCash nor any of the digital tokens that followed it were truly anonymous. Once an administrator provided a customer clear ownership rights over an asset, he or she had to record the value of that asset and the owner's name in a ledger or record. Tax, anti-money-laundering authorities and courts could force the administrator to share the ledger with them. They could force the administrator to collect know your customer (KYC) details from customers. So these digital tokens were not really anonymous.

Another shortcoming of digital currencies was that the customer had to trust their money with the administrator. The administrator could misuse the customer's money or divert the money for their own benefit and not have it available when the customer wanted it back.

In spite of the shortcomings of digital currencies, the advantages of a digital version of gold to act as a store of value appeared enticing. But the road to development of a real digital gold was blocked by two shortcomings:

1. The owner of the digital gold has to *trust a central authority* which maintained ownership and transaction records and authenticated transactions.
2. Ownership was *not confidential* because regulators could force the central authority to disclose ownership of the digital gold.

It did not take long for someone to suggest a solution – remove the central authority from the picture. Nick Szabo was a cryptographer who worked for Chaum and saw the risks of DigiCash firsthand. Being run by a company, DigiCash was open to manipulation of customer's account balances by the company.[13] In fact, any system that relied on a third party was open to such abuse. So in 1998 he proposed BitGold, a system that worked without a central authority. Szabo's key innovation was a proof-of-work protocol (we need not understand this here)[14] that allowed BitGold to be purely decentralised.

Although he figured out this solution in 1998, Szabo never really implemented it. As late as in 2008, he declared on his blog that he would like to see how his solution fared in practice and even called for volunteers to support him in coding BitGold. Satoshi Nakamoto rolled out Bitcoin later in 2008. Nakamoto has acknowledged that Bitcoin is an implementation of Szabo's BitGold proposal.[15]

Why did Bitcoin click while other digital currencies before it did not? Because Bitcoin solved a major problem that physical money faced. It was an improvement and had an instant utility.

Bitcoin is a decentralised system. The underlying technology is called Distributed Ledger Technology or DLT, because there is no central authority that maintains ledger of transactions. As a result, it is trustless and regulation-proof (a 'trustless system' is one in which there is no requirement to place trust in any third party or intermediary). It can offer both anonymity and clear ownership rights at the same time.

Now let us go back to the tax evaders (or drug dealers or arms traffickers or any economic fugitives, as the case may be) and recall their problem. If they store value in Bitcoin rather than physical cash, they have several benefits.

1. They have clear ownership rights as long as they have their private key with them. The private key is a long string of characters that can be saved in a cold wallet (pen drive) or a digital wallet and gives access to the account.
2. They retain their anonymity, as they don't have to share KYC details to own Bitcoins. Their digital identities are for everyone to see, but their real identity remains protected. Bitcoin is a peer-to-peer system without any central authority. Even if a regulator wants to clamp down on this system, it won't find a central authority to arm-twist. The regulator would have to close down all peers all over the world in order to close down the system. Remember that there are millions of peers all over the world, spread across almost all jurisdictions.
3. They are assured of their money's safety, as they do not have to trust a third party. There is no banker, no administrator, no accountant who controls the system and could try to manipulate it.

How strongly Satoshi Nakamoto believed in keeping the system trustless is evident from his white paper of 2008 introducing Bitcoin. According to him:

> Commerce on the Internet has come to rely almost exclusively on financial institutions serving as trusted third parties to process electronic payments. While the system works well enough for most transactions, it still suffers from the inherent weaknesses of the trust-based model. Completely non-reversible transactions are not really possible, since financial institutions

> cannot avoid mediating disputes. … [what] is needed is an electronic payment system based on cryptographic proof instead of trust, allowing any two willing parties to transact directly with each other without the need for a trusted third party.[16]

He never revealed his identity, probably because he feared people would see him – the inventor – as the central authority figure of the Bitcoin system. His system had no central authority.

It is also important to acknowledge that the problem Bitcoin solves is not a very ethical one. Being regulation-proof, it helps and abets tax evasion and money-laundering. Nakamoto does not mention these benefits in his white paper. Rather, he mentions other benefits:

> The cost of mediation [by financial institutions] increases transaction costs, limiting the minimum practical transaction size and cutting off the possibility for small casual transactions, and there is a broader cost in the loss of ability to make non-reversible payments for non-reversible services. With the possibility of reversal, the need for trust spreads. Merchants must be wary of their customers, hassling them for more information than they would otherwise need. A certain percentage of fraud is accepted as unavoidable. These costs and payment uncertainties can be avoided in person by using physical currency, but no mechanism exists to make payments over a communications channel without a trusted party.[17]

Reduction in transaction cost is one of the many advantages of blockchain-based cryptocurrencies. But the early adopters of Bitcoin were ones who saw its value in circumventing the law. One of the earliest use cases of Bitcoin was the Silk Road, an online marketplace for drugs and other illicit items. This marketplace could operate only because of Bitcoin. Started in 2011 by Ross Ulbricht on the darknet, it allowed buyers to pay sellers in Bitcoins. When placing an order for drugs or porn, the buyer would send money in Bitcoins to the marketplace. The marketplace worked like an escrow account and released payment to the seller once the buyer confirmed receipt of the goods. In this way, the seller remained anonymous and the only piece of information shared was the buyer's delivery location. The marketplace received a commission on each transaction. Since banks were not involved in the entire process, Silk Road could operate under the radar.

When Ulbricht started the Silk Road, he was the only seller – he listed some magic mushrooms he had grown himself. In fact, he used the Bitcoin forum for promoting his marketplace. His marketplace took off in a matter of months and acquired a million user accounts by the summer of 2013.[18] Investigators usually nab traffickers and middlemen by following the money trail. But since the money trail on the Bitcoin blockchain led to anonymous accounts, even the US government investigators could not identify Ulbricht for a long time and he could operate with impunity. A careless act he committed in initial days of Silk Road led the cops to him – he had advertised Silk Road on the Bitcoin forum using the email address rossulbricht@gmail.com. Once Silk

Road took off, Ulbricht was careful to hide his identity. Later, when the US government was desperately trying to identify him, a special task force was formed. A tax investigator with the Internal Revenue Service (IRS), who was also a part of this task force, scoured the web to record the earliest references to Silk Road and found Ulbricht's post advertising Silk Road on the Bitcoin forum. From there, it did not take him much time to connect the dots and conclude that Ross Ulbricht was the man behind Silk Road. Had Ross not made that mistake, it would have been really difficult for the investigators to even identify him, let alone catch him.

Other early adopters of Bitcoin were bribe-takers. Literature on early adoption of Bitcoin does not provide any empirical evidence to show that bribe-takers had cosied up to Bitcoin. But it makes intuitive sense to park money in Bitcoin. Kleptocrats, who are in possession of a high amount of bribe money, try to hide their money in tax havens and control the money through a complex web of shell companies. Even then, there is no guarantee of not getting detected. After the 2008 subprime crisis, larger countries led by the G20 and OECD have tried to discipline tax havens, who have forced to share information about politically exposed persons. Periodic leaks like the Paradise Papers, Panama Papers, Pandora Papers and so on have also increased the risk of detection for people who have hidden their money in tax havens. Bitcoin and other cryptocurrencies provide a much easier channel to anonymously store their funds.

Even public servants seem to have warmed up to the idea of keeping their ill-gotten wealth in cryptocurrencies. A study by the International Monetary Fund (IMF) in March 2022 found that more crypto usage was empirically associated with higher perceived corruption.[19] In October 2022, the vigilance department of the Indian state of Odisha raided the residence of a senior engineer in the state government.[20] When the raiding team landed at his house, the engineer tried to throw his mobile phone and a few documents out of a window. But the raiding team managed to recover the phone and the documents, which proved that he had invested the graft he had received in cryptocurrencies worth ₹1.75 crore.[21] Investigators were lucky to lay their hands on the evidence because this engineer was old fashioned and kept physical records of his digital coins.

It is clear that the problems that the cryptocurrency innovation has solved are a mixed bag – there are solutions for the formal economy (which I will discuss in greater detail in the next chapter) and there are solutions for the parallel economy. But we need not be scandalised by that, and there is no need for us to pass value judgement on the morality of this innovation. Even rupee notes with photographs of Mahatma Gandhi on them are used to bribe officials, pay for drugs and fund terrorist activities. This does not diminish the utility of physical cash for the larger economy. And so is the case with cryptocurrencies. Because they (like cash) can be used for illegitimate transactions it does not mean they should not be used for legitimate ones.

Separating the Wheat from the Chaff

Cryptocurrencies can perform their unique functions because of the innovation that Nick Szabo introduced – decentralisation. Decentralisation ensures that a virtual asset is tamper-proof. Decentralisation significantly reduces the risk of fraud (a decentralised virtual asset still faces the risk of manipulation by market forces).[22] To separate innovation from fraud, we need to draw up a fraud-risk map (Table 5.1). A fully decentralised peer-to-peer token system falls under the category of 'D-token'. D-tokens are low risk, as they are largely fraud-proof. A partially decentralised token falls under the category of 'PD-token' and the degree of centralised control has to be studied to assess its risk. A token that is significantly controlled by the promoters or the admin belongs to the 'C-token' category. C-tokens are high risk. Kumbhani's BitConnect was a C-token.

Table 5.1: Risk Profiles

Token type	System	Fraud Risk
D-token	Fully decentralised	Low risk
PD-token	Significantly decentralised with limited administrative control	Medium risk
C-token	Significant promoter/admin control	High risk

The US Securities and Exchange Commission (SEC) has taken action against many virtual assets by re-characterising them as 'securities'. These are usually a subset of C-tokens, where capital is often raised from the public by selling the tokens with a promise of high returns.

Raising money from the public is universally recognised as an activity that is prone to abuse. That is why countries set up a market regulator to oversee the act of raising money from the public. In India, SEBI regulates such activities. Money can be raised through the IPO route after meticulous due diligence by the regulator. Anyone eager to raise money for collective investments has to take a licence from SEBI under the Collective Investment Scheme (CIS). An unlicensed CIS which does not take licence from SEBI thus operates illegally. The schemes that are later discovered to be Ponzi or pyramid schemes are basically unlicensed CIS.

With the advent of virtual assets, many schemers are packaging their unlicensed CIS as virtual assets. A large majority of virtual assets in vogue today are C-tokens – they are controlled by a promoter or administrator. Many of these C-tokens are unlicensed CIS. Unlicensed investment schemes are, more often than not, fraudulent. The fact that they are not regulated means that the scheme's promoter can divert investments in any manner they like.

So how do we recognise this dangerous subcategory of C-tokens? Fortunately, there is a test called the Howey Test that helps us identify unlicensed CIS from among C-tokens. The Howey Test was developed by the US Supreme Court to determine if a financial instrument qualifies as an 'investment contract'. If the financial instrument passes the test, it is considered a security and should be regulated by the securities regulator (in India that is SEBI). When applied to cryptocurrencies, Howey Test identifies those virtual assets which should be licensed as investment schemes. If they are not licensed, investors are at the mercy of the schemes' promoters and crypto-enthusiasts must stay away from such virtual assets. Investing in these kinds of virtual assets is akin to giving money to a stranger you met at the train station and don't know if you will ever meet again.

Howey Test

In a landmark decision in 1946 in the case of *Howey*, the US Supreme Court laid down a few criteria to determine if an instrument was an 'investment contract'. This test is important because many times an investment contract is coloured as a different kind of a scheme. Howey test looks into the economic realities and thus unveils the substance of the scheme.

A scheme is an investment contract when 'the scheme involves an investment of money in a common enterprise with profits to come solely from the efforts of others'.[23] A particular asset should meet each of the four elements below to qualify as an investment contract:[24]

- There is an investment of money;
- In a common enterprise;
- With a reasonable expectation of profits; and
- The expectation of profits is based upon the entrepreneurial or managerial efforts of people other than the investor.

The division bench of the Allahabad High Court ruled in the case of *Paramount Bio-Tech Industries v.*

Union of India that the Howey test should be used to determine if a scheme is a 'collective investment scheme' or not. Collective investment schemes have to mandatorily register with SEBI under law. If a collective investment scheme is running without registration, it is a fraudulent scheme irrespective of whether the promoters have an intention of siphoning investors' money (more often than not, their intent is to fool investors).

Bitcoin is not an investment contract, because of multiple reasons. Investing in Bitcoin is not an investment in a common enterprise. Secondly, any expectation of profit by investors is from speculation and expectation of appreciation rather than from the entrepreneurial efforts of other people. Bitcoin miners, on the other hand, expect profit from their own mining efforts. However, many other cryptocurrencies are in the nature of investment contract.

A C-token which is not an investment fraud may still be at high risk of fraud. Consider stablecoins for the sake of illustration. Leading decentralised virtual assets (or D-token, in our terminology) are volatile, which makes them a poor store of value. To cope with this specific problem, some people floated stablecoins which are pegged to the US dollar or another fiat currency[25] or a basket of currencies. The price of a stablecoin is based on the price of currencies in the basket. Stablecoins do not have the value proposition that decentralised virtual assets have – of being trustless. But they have the other benefit of blockchain technology – it is much faster and cheaper to transfer stablecoins than the underlying fiat currencies.

And yet, stablecoins are at a high risk of fraud. This is because they are completely unregulated. By now you must have realised that stablecoins are a bit like mutual funds. Much like the value of a mutual fund is directly related to the market value of underlying securities, the value of a stablecoin varies directly with the value of the underlying currency basket. Mutual funds use the money they collect from investors to buy the underlying securities. In a similar manner, you would expect that the promotors of stablecoin's would buy the fiat currencies from the money they receive by issuing stablecoins so as to maintain the coin-to-currency ratio at all times.

And yet, there is no law that requires stablecoins to be backed by real currency. Mutual funds are subject to rules of the market regulator, tax authorities and anti-money-laundering authorities. There is no such regulation for stablecoins.[26] Being centralised, they are under the control of a promoter. The promoter can abuse its control to divert the deposits collected by issuing stablecoins. Tether, the largest stablecoin, claims that all its deposits are backed by the US dollar. And yet, authorities believe that much of Tether's assets are held not in the US dollar but US treasury bonds, corporate bonds, municipal debt and so on.[27] Tether was fined by the Commodity Futures Trading Commission of the US in October 2021 for falsely claiming that its tokens were fully backed by US dollars.[28]

This problem arises because stablecoins are not decentralised and thus are not trustless. An investor needs to trust the person(s) collecting deposits in lieu of the tokens. To increase the confidence of investors, some stablecoins have resorted to self-regulation and enhanced transparency. Digix Gold Token (DGX) is one such stablecoin. It is pegged to gold, which is 'secured in a vault managed by a custodian company in Singapore. DGX token holders pay a management fee to cover the costs of securely storing the gold.' It is subject to regular independent audits, whose reports can be publicly verified. This helps mitigate fraud risk for DGX.

In contrast to C-tokens, D-tokens are products of a trustless system, can be transferred quickly and cheaply and face low fraud risk. PD-tokens, which we describe as significantly decentralised tokens with limited administrative control, carry a medium-to-low fraud risk. A report of Financial Action Task Force (FATF) states that different coins are at different positions on a continuum of decentralisation. For instance, 'a stablecoin arrangement may operate the stabilisation centrally, but the user interface may be distributed' amongst other independent service providers.[29] Theoretically, a stablecoin could be fully decentralised too, if both the governance and underlying assets are managed through a computer algorithm. But most popular stablecoins are far from this theoretical extreme.

An Algorithm to Categorise a Virtual Asset

We saw how cryptocurrency, and blockchain in general, is an innovation with potential to structurally change the nature of money as well as the nature of doing business. But joyriding on this valuable innovation are fraudsters and illegal investment schemes that pose as cryptocurrencies. They give all virtual assets a bad name. They also increase the fraud risk of virtual assets as a class of investments.

There are analytical tools to differentiate between different kinds of virtual assets and put them into baskets. Investment contracts are extremely high risk, and could be running illegally if not licensed by SEBI Amongst the rest, virtual assets whose system is driven by a central authority present moderate-to-high risk of fraud, but they lack the strongest value proposition of cryptos – decentralisation. Virtual assets whose system is truly decentralised present low risk of fraud.

The classification of virtual assets into buckets is also represented by the flowchart in Figure 5.2.

Figure 5.2: Classification of virtual assets

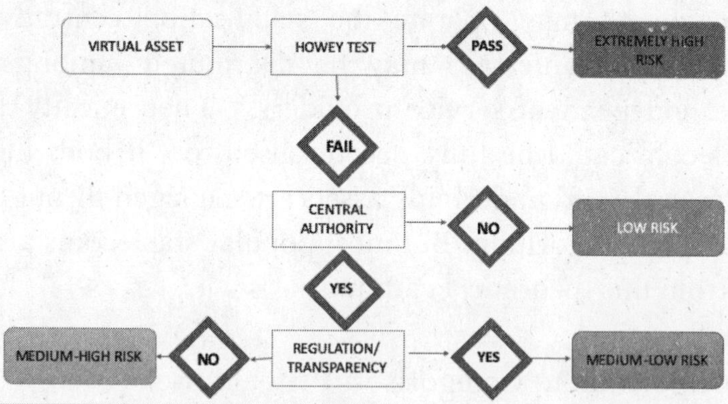

This chapter has explored the dark side of investing in virtual assets. The next chapter looks into the real innovations that the token economy is expected to herald and the surge in value creation that it brings about.

6

Crypto Elitism

Contradiction is a core concept in Marxism. Karl Marx saw society as a contradiction between social forces; change happened when these contradictions get resolved. He explained away history as a progress across timeline through resolution of contradictions between social classes. He claimed that feudal society gave way to capitalist society due to the contradictions between the feudal class and capitalist class, and he believed that the contradictions between the capitalist class and labour class would eventually give way to class conflict and revolution.

For an ideology explaining the world through contradictions, Marxism itself is full of contradictions. Marxists believe that religion is the opium of the masses. But as many sociologists have pointed out, Marxism has many elements of a religion. Another contradiction – Vladimir Lenin, who practised Marxism, had once said, 'So long as the State exists there is no freedom. When there is freedom, there will be no State.' The Russian state he formed after the Bolshevik revolution of 1917 was a totalitarian one in which the state interfered in every aspect of citizens' life.

While Marx was articulate about revolution leading to demise of capitalism, he did not clearly pronounce what political structure would come about after the revolution.

He presented a romantic idea that the revolution would lead to a dictatorship of the proletariat, which would be utopian. He saw this dictatorship of the proletariat as a peer-to-peer network, a communion, in which there was no class divide. His co-author Friedrich Engels said that the state would 'wither away' once workers controlled the means of production. But history after Marx's time is evidence of a contrary state of affairs. The state under communist regimes was autocratic, all-pervasive and too interfering in the lives of people. Rather than increasing the freedom of the people, communism significantly curtailed their freedom.

There are eerie similarities between Karl Marx and Satoshi Nakamoto of Bitcoin fame. Their ideas are revolutionary. Both have their cult followers. Marx's worldview was moulded by the effect of capitalism on the labour class after the industrial revolution. Nakamoto's worldview was affected by the financial crisis of 2008 that exposed the flaws of capitalism in current times. Both are romanticists; Marx had imagined a society which was utopian, where the capitalist class could not dictate terms to the people. Nakamoto believes in a financial system which is utopian, where governments and bankers cannot dictate monetary policy.

The similarities do not stop here. Marx wanted to snatch power concentrated with the capitalist class and give it to the masses. But Marxist revolutions led to governments that further concentrated power with autocrats and their coterie. Nakamoto had visualised Bitcoin as a purely decentralised solution to centralised banking. But centralising forces are taking over the cryptocurrency revolution. Nakamoto wanted to remove the gatekeepers of world finance – the central banks and private bankers. But cryptocurrency has led to the rise of a new class of gatekeepers.

The Gatekeepers

Sailendra Prasanna Mishra is one of those people who, at first look, you find to be clueless or absentminded, or both. On getting to know him better, you may find him ardent and eager to explain the abstruse work he does. Hailing from my hometown Bhubaneswar, the capital of Odisha state, Sailendra did a PhD researching blockchain technologies at the University of Texas at Dallas. During his PhD, he worked on questions such as whether decentralisation was sustainable in the Bitcoin system and ended up co-authoring a paper which said that 'even though the Bitcoin system is designed as an egalitarian system, it is likely to evolve into a near-centralized system because of economic forces'.[1] After his PhD, he settled in the San Francisco Bay Area (the cradle of virtual assets) and joined Lukka Tech as the director of its quant research team.

I have made few attempts to understand what research Sailendra does. I patiently engaged with him for hours, before finally giving up. If it is not easy to understand what Sailendra does, it is even more difficult to decipher what business Lukka Tech is in. Its website says that it provides 'a comprehensive, secure, and scalable technology for your crypto middle and back-office'.[2] Its clients include fund administrators, crypto native businesses, accounting firms and even regulators.

I caught up with Sailendra in Bhubaneswar during the summer of 2022 and asked him to explain why he thought that virtual asset systems could never be truly decentralised. He said that a truly decentralised crypto system was possible, but such a system would not be adopted by the masses. As with any traditional currency, a cryptocurrency's real legitimacy comes with mass adoption. But for reaching the masses, it needs to give some degree of control to centralising forces.

One major challenge that Bitcoin faced in its initial years was a slow pace of adoption. In its initial days, Bitcoin was actively embraced only by a group of techies called cypherpunks. Cypherpunks are individuals who advocate the use of technology to enhance privacy. They became an organised group when a mailing list of cypherpunks was formed in 1992 and they started conducting monthly meetings in the San Francisco Bay Area to exchange ideas. Their ideas are often political, in the sense that they believe privacy-enhancing technologies have the potential to give true freedom to people and drive social change.

Sailendra says that cypherpunks naturally embraced Bitcoin because it was the tool they needed to further their ideology, and thus the Bitcoin network became operational. But it was still a small group of techies, most of them based in the San Francisco Bay Area, who joined the Bitcoin network. It is not easy for a normal person to engage in peer-to-peer transactions or operate an unhosted wallet. Naturally, the adoption of Bitcoin was slow between 2008 and 2012. One entrepreneur, Brian Armstrong, came up with a business idea to solve this problem – make it easy for a common person to transact in Bitcoins. He started Coinbase in June 2012, which provided services such as Bitcoin-to-bank account transactions, Coinbase wallets to store Bitcoins and easy facilities to make payments using Bitcoins.

With the proliferation in virtual assets, many more service providers mushroomed. The Ethereum platform allows users to enter into smart contracts, which is touted as an important use case for virtual assets. Smart contracts can potentially remove the need for advocates and courts to enforce contracts (at least for those contracts that can be enforced through the Ethereum platform). But these smart contracts are a set of programs that run only on the Ethereum platform. If you and I are to enter into a smart contract on this platform, we may not need an advocate but we would need coders – new service providers – to develop the program.

Other service providers are custodians, mining pools, brokerage services and the exchanges that allow users to trade in virtual assets. Service providers play an important role in the crypto ecosystem – they help people without specialised coding knowledge to use virtual assets. A very unimaginative name used by regulators for such service providers is Virtual Asset Service Provider (VASP).

While VASPs have helped in increasing the adoption of virtual assets, they have become the new gatekeepers. In the process, the key promise of virtual assets like Bitcoin gets undermined. Sailendra equates a decentralised cryptocurrency to a multi-headed hydra – no one is in control, so regulators cannot manipulate any one person to exercise control on the network. But when transactions are routed through VASPs, they exercise centralised control over those transactions. As the volume of transactions through VASPs increases, so does the degree of centralisation. Sailendra says it is impossible for regulators to arm-twist peers of a network, but it is easy for them to arm-twist VASPs. VASPs are businesses, so they can be easily identified and made to collect KYC details of their clients. As a result, persons transacting in virtual assets through VASPs do not remain anonymous.

FATF, the premier international watchdog against money-laundering and terrorist financing, has been advocating a policy that seeks to regulate VASPs that act as intermediaries in virtual asset transactions. FATF has thirty-eight member countries; and with the European Commission and Gulf Cooperation Council, its membership totals forty. Yet, it has an overarching influence on almost every country in the world and uses this influence to make countries implement laws to counter money-laundering in their jurisdiction. Unlike most other international bodies (including the UN Security Council), FATF has teeth. It uses a highly technical evaluation process to place countries into baskets, and those placed in a so-called grey list basket or black list basket face economic sanctions.[3] FATF requires countries to impose the same level of KYC and anti-money-laundering requirements on VASPs as those they impose on banks and other financial institutions. In addition, VASPs are required to comply with something called the 'travel rule' that places significant burden on them to maintain records of senders and receivers of virtual assets. They are also required to report suspicious transactions to the relevant jurisdiction's financial intelligence unit (FIU).

The idea behind this policy is that most virtual asset transactions can be regulated through intermediaries. While recognising that anonymous peer-to-peer transactions via unhosted wallets would pose significant anti-money-laundering risks if mass-adopted, FATF predicts that 'there are practical and technological limitations which could mean … a radically decentralised scheme is unlikely to achieve the level of ease-of-use, security, or stability which would be necessary to achieve widespread adoption.'[4]

If FATF is successful in its plans, many virtual assets will face an existential crisis. To understand what FATF is doing, Sailendra divides all transactions in virtual assets into three types:

1. Transfer of virtual assets through intermediaries;
2. Sale or purchase of virtual assets in fiat currency (*on-ramping* refers to purchasing virtual assets by paying in rupees and *off-ramping* refers to selling virtual assets and receiving payment in rupees); and
3. Transfer of virtual assets through peer-to-peer network and through privacy enhancing tools.

A disproportionately large volume of virtual asset transactions happen through intermediaries. If a particular virtual asset is not transacted through intermediaries, it cannot achieve mass adoption. Further, both on-ramping and off-ramping will leave a money trail in bank accounts. If countries successfully regulate intermediaries, they get key data on the first two types of transactions. The risk of these transactions being used for money-laundering is, thereby, mitigated. At the same time, these transactions are no longer private.

Governments still do not have a clear visibility of peer-to-peer transactions, or transactions that use privacy enhancing tools. Mixers are digital tools that mix crypto tokens from tainted and clean sources, thus making it more difficult for investigators to identify the recipient of a particular token. But only a very small fraction of people investing in virtual assets are actually technically competent to use mixers, or to conduct a peer-to-peer transaction on the blockchain. FATF says these opaque transactions pose 'residual risk'. FATF does not perceive the volume of such transactions to be high enough to cause alarm.[5]

As of end of 2023, FATF's policies have not affected the world of virtual assets significantly. Whenever a country imposes anti-money-laundering or KYC regulations on VASPs in line with FATF standards, VASPs tend to migrate to a more liberal jurisdiction (mostly to tax havens) and take advantage of regulatory arbitrage. But FATF has the mandate and force to cajole countries to apply its standards. When FATF manages to arm-twist all major tax havens to accept its regulatory policies, intermediaries will have no option but to collect client data and compromise client anonymity. The unique selling proposition of many virtual assets – their anonymity – will then be lost. A vast majority of virtual assets will face an existential crisis. For other virtual assets, their fair market value will take a haircut.

While some see regulations as an existential threat to cryptocurrencies, others see regulation as a good thing. R. Venkatesh, head of Public Policy at CoinSwitch Kuber, a Bengaluru-based cryptocurrency exchange backed by Tiger Global and Sequoia Capital, believes that the whole idea of anti-money-laundering and KYC regulation is to maintain a certain degree of pseudonymity, below prescribed thresholds, but deter and prevent unscrupulous players from misusing virtual assets. A consistent advocate of virtual assets, he has been a good source of insight on virtual asset regulations for me. He strongly believes that more transparency through anti-money-laundering regulations will help the crypto industry thrive.

Venkatesh's core argument is that 'best should not be the enemy of good'. Full privacy may be the best option, but it is prone to abuse. So a middle path needs to be found. He says that a majority of people today want to trade and invest in virtual assets as an asset class. They will benefit from greater transparency. Those who use virtual assets as a channel for illegitimate activities, would be dissuaded and disincentivised by anti-money-laundering regulations. But then, what value do virtual assets as an asset class bring to the table if devoid of privacy-enhancing features? It is well acknowledged that there are utility coins and stablecoins, which create a different kind of value. But what about the others? Venkatesh's opinion may be tempered by his position as head of public policy of a leading VASP business. Or maybe not. It will be interesting to compare the crypto exchanges staying back and those migrating to a liberal regulatory regime after a country implements FATF standards.

Even if we consider FATF standards a threat, they would not be the severest of problems to virtual assets due to the involvement of gatekeepers. Privacy is not the only promise of virtual assets. Decentralisation is not a means to an end. Decentralisation is the end in itself. The purpose of Bitcoin – a world-changing innovation – was to introduce money that could not be controlled by anyone. Many virtual assets that came after Bitcoin were sold on the promise of being trustless systems. When there are gatekeepers, users need to trust them. Gatekeepers can commit fraud (such as the FTX fraud of 2022, which is considered as one of the top financial frauds of all times), or engage in insider trading. Fraud can be committed on gatekeepers (as seen from the way hackers have managed to steal virtual assets from exchanges). To prevent frauds, central banks and market regulators can assume jurisdiction and dictate how gatekeepers manage their affairs. Central banks could use this opportunity to further their own monetary policy goals. Nakamoto's grand plan of having a trustless system to operate money will then end up as old wine in a new bottle.

On the problem with intermediaries, Don and Alex Tapscott observed in their 2016 book, *Blockchain Revolution*:

> In the pre-blockchain world, trust in transactions derived from individuals, intermediaries, or other organisations acting with integrity. Because we often can't know our counterparties, let alone whether they have integrity, we've come to rely on third parties not only to vouch for strangers, but also to maintain transaction records and perform the business logic and transaction logic that powers commerce online. These powerful intermediaries – banks, governments, PayPal, Visa, Uber, Apple, Google and other digital conglomerates – harvest much of the value.[6]

The Tapscotts have immense faith in the trust protocol of blockchains. But transactions in the post-blockchain world are also majorly done through intermediaries. The intermediaries, the source of the ills in transactions in the pre-blockchain world, have remained. The new world has given rise to new intermediaries, new third parties we need to trust. To be fair to the Tapscotts, we have the benefit of hindsight, since much has happened between 2016 and now.

In 2022, for example, vulnerabilities of many intermediaries deeply entrenched in the virtual asset ecosystem came to the fore. Ronin, a blockchain network that operates the popular crypto game Axie Infinity, was robbed of US$625 million worth of virtual assets by North Korean hackers identified as the Lazarus group. Theoretically, virtual assets on a blockchain cannot be hacked because the same accounts are maintained on every peer's computer in the network. The hack exposed the fact that Ronin maintained centralised control over Axie Network.

In South Korea, a stablecoin by the name of TerraUSD collapsed. Stablecoins are usually pegged to fiat currency. So how can they collapse? TerraUSD was pegged to another virtual asset called Luna. Both TerraUSD and Luna were controlled by the same administrator, so was Anchor Lending Platform which offered a 20 per cent yearly return to investors for deposits made in TerraUSD coin. By offering this attractive incentive, Anchor raised the demand for TerraUSD, which in turn raised the demand for Luna. The rise in price of Luna was, therefore, artificial. Anchor never revealed how it would make money to pay such a high interest to investors.

One day, a few investors tried to withdraw about US$2 billion worth of TerraUSD from Anchor, which created panic among other investors. As a result, traders started selling TerraUSD at a discount, which ultimately led to the collapse. Although working on the Terra blockchain, TerraUSD, Luna and Anchor Lending Platform could be manipulated to create a nexus that pumped up the price of Luna. Large financial frauds are mostly perpetuated through related party transactions since the same set of shareholders exercise control over the parties. So what happened with Terra and Luna should not be surprising. But the surprise part was that they were running on the Terra blockchain, which should have been free of any administrator control.

The year 2022 ended with FTX, a leading cryptocurrency exchange, unravelling. Its failure wiped out investor wealth totalling over US$150 billion.[7] Investment firms that had virtual assets as a major share of their portfolio, such as Voyager Digital, Celsius Network and Three Arrows Capital, went bankrupt in the same year.[8] The problem of trusting intermediaries in a post-blockchain world was thus not as apparent in 2016 as it is today. As in the pre-blockchain world, investors and customers still have to rely on the integrity of intermediaries and other gatekeepers. This fact was evident when FTX went bust and the crisis spread through the entire sector.

FTX was a virtual asset trading platform and exchange founded in 2019 by Sam Bankman-Fried and Gary Wang and was registered in Antigua, a tax haven. Its senior management consisted of the two co-founders and Nishad Singh. The company lacked governance controls, board oversight, financial controls and accounting controls. It did not have employees in key positions required to monitor and control a company of its size.[9] In spite of executing complex financial operations, it did not have an enterprise resource planning (ERP) software to record transaction details. FTX had many sister concerns, but these group companies were not under the control of any parent company. Rather, there were multiple holding companies which were ultimately controlled by Bankman-Fried. One such sister concern was Alameda, a crypto hedge fund directly owned by Bankman-Fried (90 per cent) and Wang (10 per cent). Alameda was a customer of FTX just like any other customer. FTX's customers were of two types – retail customers and market makers (who were professional traders).[10] An auto-liquidation process applied to all customers. In case of retail customers, if their account balance went near zero, their existing positions were automatically liquidated. Market makers were given a line of credit, meaning that they could have negative account balance. But if the negative account balance fell below a threshold, even their positions were liquidated. The auto-liquidation process did not apply to Alameda, meaning that Alameda could withdraw any amount of cryptocurrencies from the exchange. To provide this facility, Nishad Singh had made small tweaks to the software algorithm.

Alameda used this facility to withdraw huge amounts of funds which were under the management of FTX and belonged to other customers. The funds withdrawn were then allegedly used to fund various expenses, including personal expenditure of the co-founders. Due to the large withdrawals by Alameda, FTX's balance sheet showed US$9 billion liabilities and just US$900 million in liquid assets. The balance sheet was leaked in November 2022, which revealed the low liquidity of FTX and its significant related-party transactions with Alameda. This created a panic in the market and customers started withdrawing their money from the exchange. Obviously, the exchange didn't have enough funds to pay the customers. It stopped withdrawals and filed for bankruptcy.

Most frauds in the crypto ecosystem are of the nature of investment frauds (Ponzi schemes or pyramid schemes). But the FTX fraud was a corporate fraud. The promoters used related party transactions to divert funds, which has been seen in many cases of corporate frauds. There was absolutely no regulatory oversight, even though Antigua and Barbuda, the country where the firm was located, had passed a Digital Asset Business Act in 2020 making the Financial Services Regulatory Commission its regulator and supervisor for virtual asset service providers. FTX was the second largest exchange of the world (after Binance) just before it went bust.

Which are the virtual assets that will survive the return of intermediaries? It would be the ones that have true utility. Sailendra says most tokens that take pride in being trustless systems, but do not create any other value, will fade. The few that will survive will be the ones that have the power of network effects. Virtual assets that cross a threshold of network effects will get the status of digital gold and will remain valuable even if there is no underlying value.

Whither Blockchain Revolution?

When I met Sailendra in the summer of 2022, a new tax regime for virtual assets had just been introduced in India. The new regime taxed trading gains, but did not allow setting-off of trading losses. It required VASPs to withhold tax of 1 per cent of the value of every transaction done through them. It also prescribed onerous reporting requirements for VASPs. Many VASPs migrated out of India and transaction volumes reduced significantly. The journalists and press termed this as the 'Crypto Winter'. Nevertheless, the sentiments about virtual assets among the youth were positive and there was a lot of interest about cryptos even in smaller cities like Bhubaneswar.

One day I picked up Sailendra and drove down to Konark. On the way, we discussed a recent crypto scam in a remote part of Odisha about which there was much chatter. In this scam, a lady by the name of Diana approached an engineer working in Balangir district through a group in the social media Telegram and encouraged him to invest in Bitcoins. She (we don't know who the real person was, or the person's gender) made him register on binance.com, a reputed intermediary for virtual assets, and buy Bitcoins. Then she made him open an e-wallet with an obscure website, coinfu.2020.com, and keep all the Bitcoins he had bought in this e-wallet, on the promise of high returns. The victim invested Bitcoins worth ₹3 lakh in this e-wallet over a two-month period, but when the victim asked to withdraw the money, Diana vanished. Sailendra told me how easy it had become, due to social networks, to reach out to gullible individuals and con them. Diana did not have to physically meet her (his?) victims, or even be in the same country, to perpetrate the fraud.

We headed to the marine drive between Konark and Puri. The sea was quiet and there was not much traffic on the road – most tourists landing at Bhubaneswar airport are pilgrims and catch the direct road to Puri to visit the Lord Jagannath temple. We stopped at a place where we found a fisherman frying fresh fish in a shack. We purchased fried fish and prawns and sat down by the sea. Sailendra said he was emotional about the fish harvested in Puri and would happily pay a premium if he could find it in the US. But there was no mechanism by which he could ascertain if a packet of fish claimed to be from Puri was actually from there.

Blockchain technology could develop a mechanism to authenticate the source. And such a solution would help law enforcement agencies as well, he quipped. Country of origin fraud, or simply origin fraud, was a colossal problem for customs authorities all over the world. Imports from one country were often fraudulently marked as imports from a third country (with which the importing country had a free-trade agreement) to escape import duties. To discourage this fraud, many importing countries required additional checks and documentation – bureaucratic requirements that reduced the ease of doing trade. If the entire supply chain was recorded on an immutable blockchain, customs authorities could quickly check the value addition on an import consignment in different countries and clear the goods. It would be a win-win for customs authorities as well as traders.

There are many more applications of blockchain in regulatory technology or RegTech. Being a career civil servant, I have come across powerful ideas that seek to use blockchain to increase the efficiency of governance functions. Blockchain can be used in maintaining land records (bad record-keeping leads to disputes and litigation), in authenticating transactions (so that tax administrations don't have to intrusively investigate the genuineness of a transaction) and even in drawing up contracts (the government and citizens signing smart contracts). Blockchain can also help in protecting national security related documents. I do not dispute the potential of blockchain technology in revolutionising every facet of life. But I want to understand the utility of cryptocurrencies and not the underlying technology.

Sailendra listed a few utilities of cryptocurrencies – faster and cheaper payments, and use of some cryptocurrencies as native tokens in a blockchain system that has utilities. He said that cryptocurrencies have the potential of improving payment of funds. At the same time, there are other solutions that can do this. India's United Payments Interface (UPI), that executes payments in a matter of seconds, shows how fund payments can be made, fast and cheap, using existing technologies.

There are wide swathes of the world population that are unbanked, reasoned Sailendra, and cryptocurrency can be their medium for storing wealth or making payments. According to the World Bank's Global Findex Report 2021, more than 1.4 billion adults across the world were unbanked, and 54 per cent of the unbanked lived in seven countries – China, India, Pakistan, Indonesia, Bangladesh, Egypt and Nigeria.[11] At first glance, the potential for the use of cryptocurrencies by the unbanked population looks huge. Yet, with my governance experience, I look at the proposition with some degree of scepticism. Most unbanked adults in India do not have a bank account not because of lack of banking facilities but because they do not have enough money to keep in the bank. The Global Findex Report, which is released annually, had noted in 2011 that only 35 per cent of Indian adults had bank accounts. In 2017, this increased to 80 per cent of India's adult population, which means bank adoption more than doubled in these six years. And yet, 48 per cent of account holders in 2017 had inactive accounts, meaning there was neither any deposit nor any withdrawal for over 12 months. The Global Findex Report 2017 observed that this might be because of India's Jan Dhan Yojana, which sought to improve banking penetration by opening zero balance accounts for the poor.[12] Though these citizens had Jan Dhan accounts, they did not engage in any transaction, because they did not have enough money to keep in bank accounts. In some countries, banking infrastructure is non-existent due to internal conflict, thus necessitating use of informal channels of remittance such as the age-old hawala system. Some people in such a situation may shift to cryptocurrencies. But such population would be a small fraction of the total unbanked population.

Virtual assets are also seen as a solution for faster and easier cross-border payments. They are touted to be cheaper substitutes of the SWIFT (Society for

Worldwide Interbank Financial Telecommunication) system for making cross-border payments. But many experts have acknowledged that virtual assets do not solve the problem with SWIFT that leads to delay in transactions.[13] One area where virtual assets have a definite edge is payment transactions requiring privacy. Bitcoin transactions are pseudonymous (meaning that while the identity of the wallet containing a Bitcoin is known to everyone, the identity of the individual owning the wallet is not known), and are more difficult to track than a bank transaction. There are other solutions, such as privacy coins, which ensure anonymous transactions. But who needs this high level of privacy? Drug dealers, paedophiles, money launderers, terrorists, the corrupt – who else? The cypherpunks value privacy because it gives absolute freedom to people – it is an ideological stand. But the common person is not so bothered about privacy. When I was a kid, means of communication were limited, and people used to share emotion-filled messages through postcards. These were cards anyone could read, and you can be sure the local postman knew much about my family's internal affairs than he cared to exhibit. That did not bother my parents, who would not shell out the extra twenty-five paisa to buy a postal envelope (a postal envelope gave privacy). The common person does not value privacy as a feature any more even now. In early 2021, when WhatsApp changed its privacy policy to reduce the standard of privacy on the app many privacy enthusiasts were not happy with the change. There was an uproar and there were predictions that users would shift to other instant chat applications. But that did not happen.

So, privacy is a valuable service, but only to a few. Privacy is fundamental to those involved in illegal and unethical activities and that is why privacy coins will remain valuable. Privacy coins such as Monero and Zcash have found wide usage in darknet marketplaces precisely because of features that allow anonymity of persons involved in a transaction. They have also been subject to backlash by regulators. In many countries, exchanges do not trade in privacy coins as they do not meet anti-money laundering and KYC requirements.[14]

With these coins, we see a clear trade-off that a virtual asset has to face. If it provides anonymity as a service, it would not be mass-adopted (as intermediaries subject to KYC requirements cannot facilitate transactions). If it intends to be mass-adopted, it has to shed its anonymity features. Privacy coins have decided to cater to the niche clientele of criminals and launderers, at the expense of mass adoption. The utility they provide is clear and so they have a promising future. Yet, they may not be a suitable asset class to invest in, because there is a high chance of regulatory action against privacy coins in the future. As usage of privacy coins by criminals increases, citizens in many countries may even be barred from legally owning them. Without legitimate buyers, or trades on legitimate exchanges, law-abiding citizens holding privacy coins may then feel trapped.

The second utility Sailendra alluded to was the use of virtual assets as native tokens in blockchain platforms that have other utilities. One major utility of blockchains is in development and execution of smart contracts. This is provided by some blockchain-based platforms. The largest such platform is Ethereum. Its native token,

Ether, is second only to Bitcoin in popularity. Ethereum was introduced in 2013 by a nineteen-year-old Vitalik Butelin through a white paper titled 'Ethereum: The Ultimate Smart Contract and Decentralised Application Platform'. His innovation was, to put it simply, a marriage between Bitcoin and platform economics. Ethereum is a blockchain platform on which developers can develop decentralised applications or DApps. For running the applications, developers need to enter into smart contracts on the blockchain. There is, however, a problem here. Developers can choke the system by spamming it with smart contracts.[15] To discourage this, there is a condition that anyone willing to enter into a smart contract has to use 'gas', which they can buy using Ether.

While the Bitcoin blockchain only facilitates transactions, the Ethereum blockchain allows users to develop applications. When a user develops their own application on the Ethereum blockchain, they can also develop their own tokens to work on their application. Once fully developed, such applications can run in an autonomous fashion, following the rules of the smart contract. The developers can then surrender control and make the applications truly decentralised.

These features have facilitated the development of decentralised finance or DeFi. In a typical DeFi, Sailendra explains, the administrative rules are coded into a smart contract. An app is developed based on this smart contract. Administrative rules may mandate financial transactions within the app in Ether, or in its own native token. Imagine a casino that has its own rules on how to gamble. You exchange your money for the casino's tokens when you wish to play. You play by the casino's rules to make or lose money. At the end, if you make some money, you exchange the tokens for money and exit the casino. A DeFi App (which is a type of DApp) is quite similar, except that there is no intermediary. The rules are automated and developers have willingly given up control over the app to make it truly decentralised. The DeFi App may operate any kind of financial instrument using its native token or Ether. The speciality of DeFi Apps is that there is no intermediary (other financial instruments involve intermediaries such as banks, investment managers, mutual fund firms and so on, who take a cut of your profits from the financial venture), due to which all surplus value comes to you.

Now this is extraordinary. This is also the promise of Ethereum. It is the platform to kill all platforms. In the first three chapters of this book, we saw how digital platforms disrupted pipeline businesses and drove their gatekeepers out of business. Digital platforms are now being seen as the new gatekeepers and DApps intend to drive them out of business. This reminds me of Schumpeter's theory of creative destruction, which states that new innovations will replace existing products that are obsolete. But look at the pace of such disruption – the internet revolution is only three decades old and the platform revolution started two decades ago. And we are already eyeing new innovations to disrupt them.

Mahesh Kuppannagari, a classmate and currently head of products and advisory at Ambit Global Private Client, the wealth management arm of Ambit, strongly believes in blockchain's ability to disrupt platforms. He views platforms as exploitative; the platform is at the centre of the network while its users, customers and partners are at the periphery. He sees an alternative in open platforms where users, customers and partners are empowered and made central to the network and value creation from the network. Such open platforms are possible if blockchain technology is used to automate away the administrator of the platform.

Whether DApps will be able to displace digital platforms and bring in decentralised utopia, only time will tell. But by now, some major shortcomings of smart contracts have come to light, due to which it appears that DApps may not be displacing most digital platforms anytime soon. First, smart contracts are rigid; once they are operational, there is not much room for making changes. Compare a DApp cab aggregator with Uber. If drivers or riders find loopholes in Uber's software and try to misuse it, Uber quickly adapts and makes changes to plug the loopholes. But a DApp cab aggregator won't be able to do this. In real life, there are many contingencies and uncertainties that a business has to face and adapt to. DApps have severe limitations in doing so.

Second, a smart contract may suitably simulate a transactional contract, but it is difficult for a smart contract to simulate a relational contract. In a contract, legal terms are interpreted in the light of context and circumstances. Lawyers subjectively see if a party to a contract has made best effort or reasonable effort (both being subjective judgements) to determine if there is a breach of the contract. Replicating such contracts on DApps is difficult. However, DeFi applications such as derivatives have taken off because they involve transactional contracts and can be easily replaced by smart contracts.

Third, and most importantly, not all users have a good understanding of smart contracts. The world is divided between those who understand smart contract codes (crypto elites) and those who do not. Give me a legal contract today, and I can use my general intelligence to review it to get a sense of whether it sufficiently incorporates the deal that resulted in the contract. But if you give me thousands of lines of code, I will be helpless. A Harvard Law School paper observes:

> A key challenge in the widespread adoption of smart contracts is that parties will need to rely on a trusted, technical expert to either capture the parties' agreement in code or confirm that code written by a third party is accurate. While some analogize this to hiring a lawyer to explain 'the legalese' of a traditional text-based contract, the analogy is misplaced. Non-lawyers typically can understand simple short-form agreements as well as many provisions of longer agreements, especially those setting forth business terms. But a non-programmer would be at a total loss to understand even the most basic smart contract and is therefore significantly more beholden to an expert to explain what the contract 'says'.[16]

Parties to a smart contract have to completely rely on their coders and trust that the coders have duly incorporated their understanding in the contract. Mass adoption of smart contracts has not happened precisely because of this skill divide between coders and others.

While DApps may not meet the lofty targets of disrupting platform businesses, they will be increasingly used to execute simpler autonomous applications. DeFi applications have picked up significantly. Thus, the utility of platforms like Ethereum is evident and the value of the native tokens is intricately linked with their utility.

Gold, Bitcoin, Ether

All that glitters is not gold. All that is on a blockchain is not Bitcoin. Or is it?

Gold is a store of value, even though it does not have any economic value. It has been the medium of exchange for more than 4,000 years (even more, by some estimates). It is the gold standard (obviously), meaning that currencies are pegged to gold. It was the universal standard for currencies till 1971 when the US government stopped the direct international convertibility of dollar and gold. Even today, gold is a significant part of the reserves of central banks around the world. It is an asset class no one disputes and everyone believes in.

Why does gold have so much hold over people, disproportionate to the inherent value or utility of the metal? We may say it is because gold, unlike other metals, is scarce. It is a stable and solid metal. It is immutable – for hundreds of years, alchemy (the pseudo-science of converting other base metals into gold) was a serious pursuit, though none of the alchemists ever succeeded in making gold. But why does the common person believe such properties make gold a suitable store of value? People believe in gold because of network effects. In the early days, gold had to compete with other objects as a store of value and a medium of exchange. Cowrie shells, silver, copper, bronze, leather and so on were other objects that were used as either money or store of value or both. Over time, due to the competitive advantages of gold, it became acceptable to more and more people in small societies. Civilisations were less connected in those days, but traders from one society introduced gold in other societies. More and more people started accepting gold's value across societies. As the number of people believing in gold increased, network effects kicked in and its value increased exponentially.

Something similar seems to be happening with Bitcoin. It has all the competitive advantages that gold has – scarcity, stability, immutability – but so do many other virtual assets. The edge Bitcoin has is in the network effects that it has managed to harness. The number of public addresses of Bitcoin users stood at 50 million in October 2023; more than 62.5 per cent of Bitcoins were held by users for more than one year, while 44.6 per cent and 32.3 per cent of all Bitcoins were held by users for more than 2 and 3 years, respectively.[17] This is early evidence of the trust users repose in Bitcoin as a store of value. It is used as a medium of exchange only in the dark web, El Salvador and the Central African Republic. Nevertheless, it is widely accepted as a store of value across the world.

The value of Bitcoin will keep rising with the size of its network. Its 'developers, users, miners, merchants, and exchanges, among others, drive the network effect that creates its … moat and unique prominence'[18] due to which no copycat virtual asset can beat it or come close to it. As we saw earlier, network effects help the winner take all.

It should, however, not be concluded that Bitcoin is the only virtual asset that can take advantage of network effects. It will be difficult for another virtual asset in the same product class to grow and survive, but a virtual asset from another product class can grow and prosper using the benefits of network effects.

This is exactly how Ether is growing. It is the native token of Ethereum, the platform for decentralised applications. Its platform provides a different kind of incentive to developers and users to connect. Figure 6.1 maps the growth in unique addresses of Bitcoin and Ethereum blockchains (which can be used as a proxy for users of the network) from 2016 to 2022. The number of users of Bitcoin has been rising consistently and quite linearly at a slope of 20 degrees. The Ethereum platform was released in 2015 with much hype among tech elites. And yet, the network did not gain significant number of users until the beginning of 2018. Its network took off in 2018 and has been steadily expanding (the expansion is linear, at a slope of about 7 degrees).

Figure 6.1: Unique addresses of users of Bitcoin and Ether

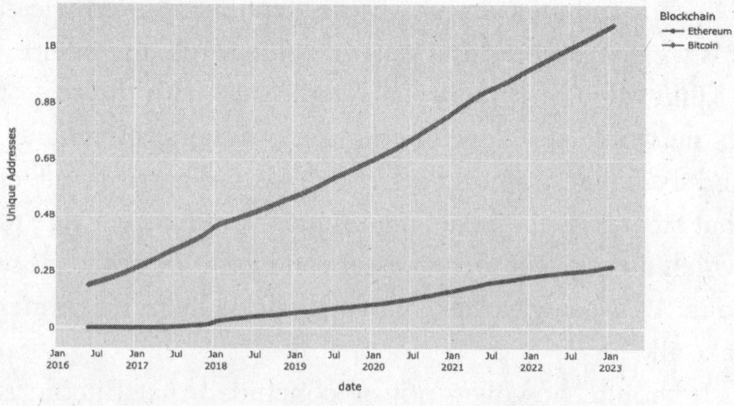

Data source: Coinmetrics.in

Figure 6.2: Transaction count of Bitcoin and Ether over time

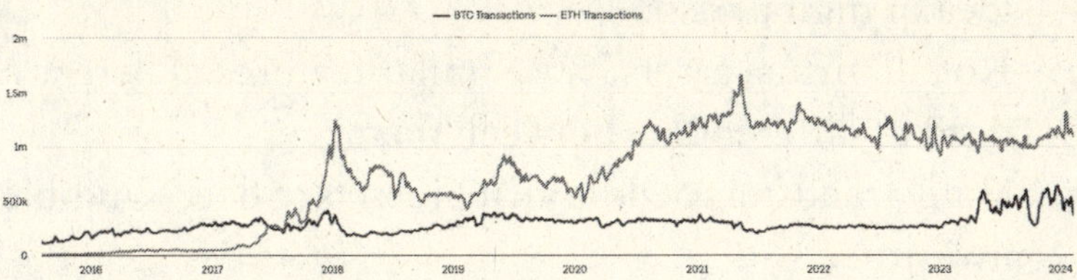

Source: The Block (theblock.co)

That Bitcoin and Ether belong to two different product categories is evident from the fact that even though Ether has a much smaller network than Bitcoin, it is more frequently transacted (Figure 6.2). Bitcoin has been a good store of value, but its use as a medium of exchange is limited to contraband items on the darknet. The frequency of daily transactions has remained consistent between 2016 and 2022. Ether, on the other hand, is used as a medium of exchange by developers and users on the Ethereum platform. As engagements on DApps, Non Fungible Tokens (NFT) and smart contracts have increased, so has the use of gas (which you get by spending Ether).

An interesting observation from Figure 6.2 is the flat line of Bitcoin's daily transactions. A zero slope shows that the darknet economy has stagnated in this period (if transactions can be considered as a proxy for economic activity). While we do not have statistics indicating the size of the darknet economy, Bitcoin usage is a good indication to understand how this underground economy is performing.

In summary, the previous chapter and this one try to make the following points:

1. Blockchain technology is revolutionary and so is the idea of digital cash.
2. Not all virtual assets have similar features. There is a need to differentiate between them.
3. Many fraudsters peddle virtual assets to fleece gullible investors.
4. Many virtual assets are in the nature of securities and should ideally be regulated. But they are not regulated in many countries. So the risk of fraud is high.
5. The risk of VASPs defaulting is also high, because the sector is new and supervision over VASPs has not matured. The FTX debacle is a good example of this.
6. Virtual assets generally have limited utility. Privacy in transactions is one, but there is a trade-off between high privacy and high adoption.
7. Blockchain-based platforms have many utilities, which will increase in the coming years.
8. Not all virtual assets will survive. Those that will survive and prosper, and may go on to become digital versions of gold, are the ones which can take advantage of network effects.

Virtual Asset Sector in India

When this book went to press, virtual assets were not regulated in India. There have been multiple debates and discussions on whether to regulate virtual assets or to summarily ban them. On 6 April 2018, the RBI prohibited entities regulated by it to deal in VAs or provide services for facilitating any person or entity in dealing with or settling VAs through a circular. This circular was quashed by the Supreme Court on 4 March 2020. In the meantime, on 22 July 2019, the government released a draft Banning of Cryptocurrency & Regulation of Official Digital Currency Bill, 2019. While this bill was not tabled in the legislature, a new bill – Cryptocurrency and Regulation of Official Digital Currency Bill, 2021 – was released by the government on 19 January 2021. This new bill sought to 'create a facilitative framework for creation of the official digital currency to be issued by the Reserve Bank of India.'[19] The bill also proposed prohibition of all private cryptocurrencies in India, although it also proposed to allow for 'certain exceptions to promote the underlying technology of cryptocurrency and its uses'.[20] This bill has also not been tabled in the Parliament.

To ban or to regulate – this is a question miring multiple jurisdictions. For countries like India with capital controls, legitimising cryptocurrencies can be a challenging proposition. I will illustrate this with an example of one kind of capital controls. Capital controls placed on Indian residents are detailed in the Foreign Exchange Management Act (FEMA) and associated rules made under this law. FEMA places restrictions on the free movement of capital outside the country. If a resident individual wants to make an investment or expenditure outside the country, it has to go through the 'liberalised remittance scheme' route. Further, only up to US$2,50,000 can be sent out per financial year by a person using this route. However, with the proliferation of blockchain infrastructure, an Indian resident can send value out of the country in the form of cryptocurrencies. RBI, or any other regulator, could exert control over VASPs registered in India and require them to monitor outward remittances. But Indian residents can send money out of India through private wallets as well. VASPs have no control over private wallets. It takes about five to ten minutes to create a private wallet. A resident can transfer virtual assets from their wallets hosted with a VASP to a private wallet and from there transfer the VAs to a hosted wallet of an overseas VASP, from where they can encash the money. VAs make cross-border transactions so easy and supervision-free that they can render various FEMA norms ineffective. Blind spots in India's capital controls regime can compromise the nation's economic security. Without a handle to limit the flow of foreign capital in and out of India, the economy could be exposed to too much hot money entering India and creating speculative bubbles, or too much money leaving India in a panic run, that could crash the capital markets.

Countries with liberal capital control policies do not face this challenge, but countries with high capital controls do. In this book, it is not possible to get into the merits of monetary policy, but legitimising cryptocurrencies will ultimately restrict the central bank's monetary policy choices and in times of crisis, the central bank will not be able to respond by limiting the flow of capital out of India.

At the same time, India understands the potential of virtual assets as drivers of innovation. The Bill of 2021 acknowledged this when it proposed to allow certain private cryptocurrencies to operate in India to promote the underlying technology and its uses. Thus, it is a paradoxical situation that India and its central bank find themselves in.

While India has not explicitly banned virtual assets or regulated them (it would designate a regulator when it wants to regulate virtual assets), it has followed an ad hoc approach to cope with the challenges they bring about. Through tax laws, it has sought to discourage the industry from proliferating in India. The Finance Act of 2022 provided for a 30 per cent tax on capital gains made in virtual asset transactions (with surcharge and cess, the total tax goes up to 33 per cent). However, it does not allow any deduction for capital losses. A trader would frequently buy and sell on a crypto-exchange to make a profit. The overall profit may be decent, because it is a net of gain and losses from different transactions. The tax law does not allow this netting off. Say, in 5 transactions in one year, a trader makes a gain of 10, loss of 6, gain of 2, loss of 5 and a gain of 4. The net gain in the year is 5. But a tax of 33 per cent is imposed on gross gains, that is, 16 (= 10 + 2 + 4), which works out to 5.28 – more than the net gains. This has effectively made speculative trading unviable in India. To top it, a 1 per cent withholding tax liability has been placed on VASPs for all transactions in virtual assets through them. As a result, many exchanges shut shop and migrated out of India.

Subsequently, in March 2023, India also introduced anti-money-laundering controls for service providers dealing in virtual asset transactions in a notification under the Prevention of Money Laundering Act. In this notification, VASPs in India were required to maintain

KYC records of their clients and report suspicious transactions.

Was this tax regime an indirect ban on virtual assets? It does not seem so, because a handful of VASPs continued to operate in India. The new tax regime served to discourage speculative investments in virtual assets. It did not target long term investment in them. The tax regime served to de-risk the sector by penalising high-risk transactions with unreasonably high taxes. But it did not hit genuine investors who saw popular VAs like Bitcoin and Ethereum as a new asset class and wanted to invest in them.

7

Think Networks

As with every other institution, the digital revolution has deeply affected the government. On one hand, it has helped governments bridge the gap in service delivery through e-governance solutions. On the other hand, it has opened up new areas of vulnerabilities for law enforcement authorities. Some of the earliest questions that digitalisation posed were on jurisdiction. Consider, for example, a hacker who inflicts a cyber-attack on facilities in India from Singapore. Which country has the jurisdiction to investigate it? What if the facilities are hosted on a server in Maldives, but run by an Indian business? What if the hacker is a citizen of Cyprus? What if he has been employed by a terrorist group from Pakistan to perpetuate the crime? Which countries will have jurisdiction over the case?

The international community has managed to cope with the challenge to a large extent by developing protocols for international cooperation. However, some gaps still remain. One such gap is in imposing the right amount of tax on platform companies. A lot has been done in the last few years to tackle this problem, but the problem persists. This is a very personal story for me and one in which we may find lessons on how to approach the network economy.

The problem statement is simple. How does a country tax a platform business that has no physical presence in the country?

A pipeline business operates by creating value across a supply chain. Every unit in a supply chain is allocated profits in proportion of the value it generates. Since units have physical presence wherever they do business, their respective profits will be taxed by the territory they are based in. This is called the *territorial nexus* of taxation. A country or a state can tax you only if there is a nexus between your income and its territory. This concept has developed over the last hundreds of years and has helped resolve disputes between countries and taxpayers. Ideally, Indian tax officers would love to tax Elon Musk on the profits he made by speculating on Dogecoin in the US. But they cannot, because there is no territorial nexus. If an Indian citizen leaves India and becomes a tax resident in, say, Guatemala, Indian tax officers cannot lay hands on their income from outside India. They can still charge the person's income from Indian soil to tax, since there is a territorial nexus of the income with India.

Platform businesses create value by connecting users in cyberspace. They do not need to be physically present in a country to engage with users in that country. To avoid taxes, they operate from an offshore territory that does not tax them.

Many platform businesses operate out of Ireland, for example, and do business across the globe. If we apply the principle of territorial nexus, then they are taxable only in Ireland whereas they do business in many other countries. And they have chosen Ireland because it does not tax them. Under Irish law, a company that is incorporated in Irish territory but has management and control outside Ireland does not have to pay tax in Ireland. So businesses open two companies in Ireland – an operating company and a holding company. The operating company runs the digital platform in Ireland and earns income from all over the world. It pays most of its income to the holding company as royalty for the use of intellectual property (the holding company owns the platform intellectual property). The holding company's management is based in Bermuda, so it does not have to pay tax in Ireland. This scheme was popularly called the *Double Irish*. Under pressure from the European Commission (EC), Ireland closed this scheme but immediately started a similar scheme called *Single Malt* (as you rightly guessed, the management of the holding company now moves to Malta instead of Bermuda). EC again pressurised, and Ireland closed this scheme as well and started another called *Green Jersey* (yes, the management of the holding company shifts to Jersey, another tax haven).[1]

Over time, sovereigns realised that this was a serious leakage of tax revenue that they could not plug by arm-twisting tax havens or threatening corporations. Corporations were not evading any tax, they were merely engaged in legitimate tax planning to minimise their tax payout. Sovereigns sulked when platform companies grew to have outsized market capitalisation and dominated stock markets. The matter assumed urgency when sovereigns realised that the entire economy was getting digitised. Traditional companies, which hitherto were organised on pipeline models, were restructuring their business to harness the power of digital platforms.

Tax persons wanted their share of the income, but had no jurisdiction to tax these platforms.

Many countries introduced interim measures, which primarily consisted of imposing a levy on payments made by the residents to these platforms. This was not a good method to impose income tax, as it was a levy on the gross receipts of platforms from a particular jurisdiction. Most successful platforms were owned by entrepreneurs based in the US. The US government saw these levies (called variously as 'Digital Service Tax', 'Equalisation Levy', etc.) as distortionary to digital trade and threatened retaliatory action.[2] Indeed, these measures were distortionary because they did not tax income (i.e., profit) of the platforms but their gross revenue. So these interim measures could not be a permanent solution to the problem.

While looking for a solution, many tax diplomats decided to move away from the territorial nexus. They did not see the new platform business models as the problem, rather they considered the age-old territorial nexus – from which they derived jurisdiction – as the problem. Some came up with the concept of a virtual nexus, but that did not gather much acceptance.

The OECD, which has been a key leader in driving the tax agenda internationally, came up with a solution. In May 2019 it stated that digital platforms would attribute a share of their global profits in markets where they made profit by using a formula, irrespective of whether they had physical presence there or not.[3] This idea (often called the formulaic approach) caught steam and many countries around the world came on board to negotiate and arrive at a consensus around this idea. The negotiations were led by the Task Force on Digital Economy (TFDE) at the OECD. I joined the tax diplomacy cell of India, the Foreign Tax & Tax Research Division in January 2020. At the time, it looked like history in the making – international tax norms, which were last made in 1919 by a group of four economists affiliated to the League of Nations, were being reformed after a century to cope with the challenge of digitalisation.

The proceedings were intense and challenging (since most of the work happened while COVID-19 related travel restrictions were in place), but OECD had both the expertise in the field and the mandate, which helped it to conduct the negotiations between more than a hundred countries. While the proceedings were privileged, the output of the negotiations was released for public consultation from time to time.

OECD released a blueprint of the new tax regime in October 2020,[4] which was extremely complex and appeared unwieldy. The blueprint proposed a whole new accounting standard to meticulously record the jurisdiction in which a corporation's services were actually consumed. For different kinds of digital services (such as online advertising, online intermediation platforms, online search engines, online gaming, digital content services, etc.) it proposed elaborate methods to estimate the services which were consumed in a jurisdiction.

This was a new tax universe in itself, having its own nexus rules, revenue sourcing rules, elimination of double taxation, safe harbour rules and so on. It required a business to maintain three sets of accounts – one as per international accounting standards, a second as per domestic tax rules and a third to comply with this new regime. If a single platform was providing multiple services (such as online intermediation and online gaming), it had to use different accounting styles to record the location of consumers for the different businesses.

Many experts were of the view that it was a bizarre attempt at taxing the digital economy. Suranjali Tandon, faculty at National Institute of Public Finance and Policy, wrote off the entire blueprint and said it just could not be implemented. A senior partner at a Big 4 firm explained to me that the compliance burden seemed to distinctly outweigh the tax benefits from the scheme. He wondered that if the blueprint had to make so many estimates, why not make it simpler?

To give OECD some credit, the task was not an easy one. When so many negotiators sit down to make a horse, they end up making a camel, as a colleague had once told me. But, as Tandon asked me – how could OECD have strayed so far away from the path? There were others who felt similarly.

In the early days of the negotiations, the United Nations (UN) – a rival international organisation on tax matters – had supported a proposal made by Rajat Bansal, an Indian Revenue Service officer of the 1987 batch, as a solution to the problem of not being able to tax platforms.[5] This proposal had its own problems – although simple, it had no way of determining the profit a firm received by hosting a network of users from a jurisdiction.[6] As a result, there was more popular support for the OECD approach than the UN approach. But as time passed and OECD's approach evolved, it appeared even more complex.[7] Many countries looked to the UN for a better solution. In November 2022, a resolution in the UN General Assembly gave it the mandate to lead intergovernmental talks on global tax rules.[8]

While an efficient solution to the issue is not in sight as of early 2024, I have often pondered over why OECD's solution was so complex. The OECD model, on which the best tax experts from around the world worked, was beautiful, meticulous and logical. The criticism was that it was too complex and unwieldy. Why? Probably because the people who contributed to it tried to solve a *new problem* in the same *old way*. The old tax system was good to tax pipeline businesses, but it could not catch platform businesses within its net. The problem arose with an innovation – the digital platform. But tax officials saw it as a problem arising from the territorial nexus. The thinking was still 'pipeline' and not 'network'.

OECD's blueprint recast multi-sided markets as companies providing automated digital services. That is why there were many different rules based on the type of service provided by a digital company. The blueprint meticulously identified the different kinds of 'services' that platform companies provide and made elaborate rules (for each service) to find which country the consumer of such services was located in. Thus a problem arising from networks was addressed with a solution for pipelines. And so, while making a horse, OECD ended up making not a camel but an octopus.

This is a challenge that businesses, not just policymakers, also face when analysing networks. Among entrepreneurs, the ones who understood network effects have succeeded, while many who could not understand network effects have burnt their fingers. Investors who really understand network effects have made the right investment decisions; others have lost money. There is a plethora of advice and literature on network effects in public forums, and people swear by it, but few are actually successful in interpreting them. OECD also knew the dynamics of network effects,[9] but its solution was influenced by its experience with tax laws. It saw platform companies as entities that provided automated digital services. As seen from the blueprint, not one attempt was made to understand the type of the network of these platforms, or their pattern within a country and across borders. To find the optimal solution, perhaps, it had to unlearn all that it had learnt when designing policies for pipeline companies.

There is a lesson here for anyone navigating through the platform revolution (and more generally, the Industrial Revolution 4.0), for entrepreneurs, investors, managers, coders, architects, regulators and policymakers – unlearn what you know, then learn about this revolution. Keep your past learnings and experience compartmentalised when steering through digital networks.

The Crypto Way

In mid-2022, I moved from a tax diplomacy position to India's Financial Action Task Force Cell (FATF Cell) as its director. As the international watchdog on money-laundering and terrorist financing, FATF releases extensive documentation for the public on money-laundering and terrorist financing risks from different typologies. To help counter such risks, it requires countries to implement its standards (called the FATF recommendations). When I deep-dived into FATF's public releases of the last few years, I realised the manner in which cryptocurrencies had disrupted FATF's approach to mitigating the risks from money-laundering and terrorist financing.

FATF broadly divides transactions in cryptocurrencies into two types – those that happen through intermediaries and those that happen between peers without an intermediary. It has a strategy for the risks arising out of the first type of transactions, but it lacks a clear strategy for mitigating the risks from peer-to-peer transactions in cryptocurrencies.[10]

The strategy for the first type of transactions is to force intermediaries to be transparent. But it is easy for intermediaries to move from one country to another. Any rule to regulate intermediaries in crypto transactions cannot be successful unless all countries, including tax havens, uniformly implement the same rule. This is a challenge of byzantine proportions.

Cryptocurrency technology also nullifies the effect of many reforms FATF has pushed for years. For example, FATF supports beneficial ownership transparency by nudging countries to maintain beneficial ownership information. The idea is to help law enforcement authorities easily detect the beneficial owners of shell companies and haven-based trusts, who are usually kleptocrats. But cryptocurrencies like Bitcoin are pseudonymous. Some, like Monero, are anonymous. Kleptocrats need not create an elaborate chain of companies in tax havens to hide their money; they can instead store Bitcoin in a cold wallet (this is a physical storage of the size of a pen drive, used to store Bitcoins offline). They may receive bribe payments in Bitcoins merely by accepting a cold wallet from the bribe-payer, thus eliminating the arduous problem of receiving and moving cash. With virtual assets, it has become even easier to hide wealth without revealing beneficial ownership.

A second example is FATF's work on supervision of non-profit organisations (NPOs). FATF's argument is that NPOs may be misused by raising donations through them from terrorist sympathisers, or by using the NPO's corpus to fund radicalisation or terrorism. Having recognised the misuse of some NPOs for terrorist financing, FATF has recommended that countries identify high risk NPOs and take appropriate measures against them. Now cryptocurrency has made it much easier to raise and use donations for terrorist financing. An organiser can now reach the target population across geographies through social networks. They can radicalise users located far and wide and collect donations from them. The organiser does not have to incorporate any legal entity to collect donations; they merely need a wallet to accept donations. They do not face any capital controls or regulatory supervision when raising donations from across the border. They pose as good Samaritans engaged in crowdfunding for a social project, but the money collected in the wallet would ultimately be used for funding terrorist activities. Such modes of raising terrorist finance are much easier than using NPOs and so will be preferred in the future.

FATF will have to come up with implementable solutions to tackle these new risks arising from cryptocurrency usage. One simple solution is to completely ban virtual assets. But then, these assets are just a ledger shared and stored in a network. A country may ban virtual assets, but it cannot ban a network of users. Such a ban would never be effective, because it is impossible to raise a cyber police force to patrol and discipline user networks. A ban will only push intermediaries underground without actually mitigating any money-laundering or terrorist financing risk.

The next best alternative is to regulate intermediaries. But given the cross-border nature of crypto-networks, any attempt at regulation will be effective only if it is implemented uniformly across jurisdictions.

Thus, the international community needs to think fast and, more importantly, needs to think in terms of networks in order to come up with efficient solutions for the problems arising from virtual assets.

Epilogue

The art of science communication is to explain how things happen and let readers draw their own conclusions. Communicating technologies is probably a tad different from science communication. This is because the communicator also has to explain how technologies are bringing about change. And there are multiple facets to the changes that technology heralds.

In this book, I have delved into the economics of internet technology and my approach has been to judge value creation. This is an approach I am comfortable with. But there are other equally appropriate approaches to see the changes technology brings. To cite an example, I was recently having coffee with two friends who work in tech. They explained to me how ChatGPT and Bard, and artificial intelligence (AI) generally, are changing the world. AI is general purpose technology and will perform many jobs that humans are performing today. People will lose jobs. My friends acknowledged that AI has not reached a level where it can holistically interpret legal statutes or give innovative solutions, but it can write codes and essays. And the speed at which AI is developing capability is stupendous. My friends were concerned about it.

When we approach the issue from the perspective of value creation, we see the problem differently. AI is going to increase the productivity of services manifold. The third industrial revolution helped increase the productivity of manufacturing. More automation meant higher productivity. In countries where development was driven by the manufacturing sector, a rise in productivity led to more exports and thus more income. But automation did not increase the productivity of services. Services faced another issue – they could not be exported like goods. Since most services could not be performed remotely, export of services required people to move across countries, which is not possible due to immigration controls. So countries which relied on services for growth had to contend with a limited growth rate.

AI is going to change all that. AI will increase the productivity of services. What one lawyer did with, say, a team of four paralegals, will be done by the lawyer alone, with a smart AI solution. The lawyer will still need to supervise the AI solution's output. But the lawyer's productivity will increase manifold, since they will be doing their own job as well as that of the paralegals. Similarly, a teacher can prepare more detailed study material for a classroom in the same time as earlier with the help of AI.

More productivity in services will mean services would be available at lower cost – a win for customers. More productivity will also mean wealth creation for the firms developing AI solutions. Note that it is difficult to export services of paralegals, but it is easy to export AI solutions from one country to another and the AI program replacing an American lawyer's paralegals may be developed and trained in Bengaluru. Countries that back the winning firms will see galloping growth in prosperity. Interestingly, AI coupled with 5G technology also holds the promise of increasing revenues from the export of services.

While in a few decades AI will manage to take up many tasks being performed by humans now, it will still need supervision. Machines would be able to perform tasks that they learn on the job, but they would be dumb in the face of novelty. They would also need troubleshooting in case of errors. The supervision can take place remotely, which means more export of services. Like India and other countries economically benefited from BPOs (business process outsourcing), enabled by information and communication technology, they will also benefit when the job of managing AI systems is outsourced.

This ability of new technologies to improve productivity makes them extremely potent vehicles of wealth creation. As per one investment management firm's estimates, investment in AI will see a compounded annual growth rate (CAGR) of 26 per cent between 2020 and 2030. In the same period, investment in blockchain will gain a CAGR of 43 per cent and investment in robotics will gain a CAGR of 51 per cent.[1] This is the promise of the Fourth Industrial Revolution. The revolution is underway, and we are experiencing it every day. Towards the end of the revolution, when the dust settles, we will be able to see how profoundly this technological revolution has changed our society, our economy and our ways of life.

Notes

Preface

1 Ha-Joon Chang. 2011. *23 Things They Don't Tell You about Capitalism*. London: Penguin Books.

2 Smarak Swain. 2019. 'Angel Tax for Start-ups: DCF Creating a Hullaballoo?' LawStreetIndia. Available at: http://www.lawstreetindia.com/experts/column?sid=237 (accessed on 30 April 2023).

3 In investment lingo, a 10X valuation means that the value of the company is ten times its sales. This is a crude, yet simple way of communicating value. It is crude because it does not follow from any standard logic of valuation, nor does it account for profits, growth and cash flows. It shows value merely as a multiple of sales.

Chapter 1 Introduction

1 SEBI. 2021. Red Herring Prospectus, 6 July. Available at https://www.sebi.gov.in/filings/public-issues/jul-2021/zomato-limited-rhp_50950.html

2 https://www.sebi.gov.in/filings/public-issues/jul-2021/zomato-limited-rhp_50950.html

3 *ET Panache*. 2021. 'Zomato gets support from peer Swiggy; love from Oyo & Paytm bosses helped Deepinder Goyal deal with IPO pangs'. 14 July.
Available at: https://economictimes.indiatimes.com/magazines/panache/zomato-gets-support-from-peer-swiggy-love-from-oyo-paytm-bosses-helped-deepinder-goyal-deal-with-ipo-pangs/articleshow/84407764.cms?utm_source=contentofinterest&utm_medium=text&utm_campaign=cppsthttps://economictimes.indiatimes.com/magazines/panache/zomato-gets-support-from-peer-swiggy-love-from-oyo-paytm-bosses-helped-deepinder-goyal-deal-with-ipo-pangs/articleshow/84407764.cms?from=mdr

4 NDTV. 2021. 'NITI Aayog CEO to NDTV on Why Fuel Prices Can't Be Cut'. NDTV, 15 July. Available at: https://www.youtube.com/watch?v=IzbCOvf4Blo (accessed on 2 December 2023).

5 Brian McCullough. 2018. 'A Revealing Look at the Dot-Com Bubble of 2000 – And How It Shapes Our Lives Today'. ted.com, 4 December. Available at: https://ideas.ted.com/an-eye-opening-look-at-the-dot-com-bubble-of-2000-and-how-it-shapes-our-lives-today/ (accessed on 22 July 2023).

6 Jules Gray. 2015. 'The History of the Dotcom Bubble – and How It Could Happen Again'. *The New Economy*, 5 October. Available at: https://www.theneweconomy.com/technology/dotbomb-are-tech-investments-about-to-destabilise-the-economy (accessed on 22 July 2023).

7 technobuffalo.com. 2010. 'Five Dot-Coms That Did Not Survive the Bubble'. technobuffalo.com, 25 January. Available at: https://www.technobuffalo.com/five-dot-coms-that-didnt-survive-the-bubble (accessed on 3 August 2021); Investopedia. 2021. 'Why Did pets.com Crash So Drastically?' Available at: https://www.investopedia.com/ask/answers/08/dotcom-pets-dot-com.asp (accessed on 3 August 2023).

8 Rick Dagley. 2013. 'eWEEK at 30: How Amazon Survived the Dot-Com Crash to Rule the Cloud'. eWEEK, 27 December. Available at: https://www.eweek.com/cloud/eweek-at-30-how-amazon-survived-the-dot-com-crash-to-rule-the-cloud/ (accessed on 4 August 2023); Timothy B. Lee. 2017. 'The Little-Known Deal That Saved Amazon from the Dot-Com Crash'. vox.com, 5 April. Available at: https://www.vox.com/new-money/2017/4/5/15190650/amazon-jeff-bezos-richest (accessed on 4 August 2023).

9 DuckDuckGo was started in 2008. I have referred the history of search engines from the site: https://www.page1.co.uk/blog/search-engines-2000-2019/ (accessed on 30 December 2023).

10 Statistics collected from https://gs.statcounter.com/search-engine-market-share (accessed on 01 Jan 2024).

11 The search engine history was noted from https://carlhendy.com/history-of-search-engines/#google2 (accessed on 22 July 2021).

12 Saul Hansell. 2004. 'Google and Yahoo Settle Dispute Over Search Patent', *New York Times*. 10 August. Available at: https://www.nytimes.com/2004/08/10/business/technology-google-and-yahoo-settle-dispute-over-search-patent.html

13 Reghu Balakrishnan. 2014. 'Discounts Backfire; Many E-com Ventures Shut Shop'. *Business Standard*, 26 February. Available at: https://www.business-standard.com/article/companies/discounts-backfire-many-e-com-ventures-shut-shop-114022600591_1.html (accessed on 19 July 2021).

14 Suprita Anupam. 2017. 'Income Tax Department Conducts Survey at Major Bitcoin Exchanges'. Inc42, 13 December. Available at: https://inc42.com/buzz/income-tax-bitcoin-exchanges/ (accessed on 22 July 2021).

15 Cleartax. 2023. 'Income Tax on Bitcoin and Its Legality in India'. 6 June. Available at: https://cleartax.in/s/bitcoins-taxes-india; See also ETBFSI. 2022. 'Why Is RBI So Vehemently Opposed to Cryptocurrencies?' Economic Times. 16 February. Available at: https://bfsi.economictimes.indiatimes.com/news/policy/why-is-rbi-so-vehemently-opposed-to-cryptocurrencies/89594369https://bfsi.economictimes.indiatimes.com/news/policy/why-is-rbi-so-vehemently-opposed-to-cryptocurrencies/89594369

16 Marie Huillet. 2021. 'Survey: 21% of UK Crypto Investors Say They Know Almost Nothing about It'. Cointelegraph, 8 July. Available at: https://cointelegraph.com/news/survey-21-of-uk-crypto-investors-say-they-know-almost-nothing-about-it (accessed on 19 July 2023).

17 As on 30 December 2023.

Chapter 2 Platform Economics

1 As per MindGeek's data, its websites have 115 million daily active users. YouTube had 122 million daily active users in 2021 (https://www.globalmediainsight.com/blog/youtube-users-statistics/).

2 Patricia Nilsson. 2020. 'The Secretive World of MindGeek: The Montreal-Based Company behind Pornhub and RedTube'. *Financial Post*, 18 December. Available at: https://financialpost.com/financial-times/the-secretive-world-of-mindgeek-

the-montreal-based-company-behind-pornhub-and-redtube (accessed on 4 August 2021).

3 John Biggs. 2018. 'The Annual Pornhub Year in Review Tells Us What We're Really Looking at Online'. TechCrunch, 14 December. Available at: https://techcrunch.com/2018/12/13/the-annual-pornhub-year-in-review-tells-us-what-were-really-looking-at-online/ (accessed on 4 August 2021).

4 Curtis Silver. 2018. 'Pornhub 2018 Year in Review Insights Report Will Satisfy Your Data Fetish' *Forbes*, 11 December. Available at: https://www.forbes.com/sites/curtissilver/2018/12/11/pornhub-2018-year-in-review-insights-report/?sh=51334c827369 (accessed on 4 August 2021).

5 Kal Raustiala and Christopher Jon Sprigman. 2019. 'The Second Digital Disruption: Streaming & the Dawn of Data-Driven Creativity'. *New York University Law Review*. 94(6): 1555–1622.

6 Geoffrey G. Parker, Marshall W. Van Alstyne and Sangeet Paul Choudary. 2016. *Platform Revolution: How Networked Markets Are Transforming the Economy – And How to Make Them Work for You*. New York: W.W. Norton & Company.

7 Gireesh Babu. 2013. 'How Bharat Matrimony Became the Best Priest in the Marriage Business, *Business Standard*, 1 October. Available at: https://www.business-standard.com/article/companies/how-bharat-matrimony-became-the-best-priest-in-the-marriage-business-113100100016_1.html (accessed on 10 August 2021).

8 Gireesh Babu. 2013. 'How Bharat Matrimony Became the Best Priest'.

9 For instance, Jean Piaget's constructivist theory of learning stresses on engaged learning through discussions with peers as an important part of the learning process: Jean Piaget. 1969. *The Mechanisms of Perception*. New York: Basic Books; the sociologist Lev Vygotsky has shown the role of social interactions in the learning process: Lev Vygotsk. 1931. 'The Genesis of Higher Mental Functions'. Available at: https://www.marxists.org/archive/vygotsky/works/1931/higher-mental-functions.htm (accessed online on 11 August 2021).

10 NextIAS is a coaching institute started in 2017 by a breakaway group of tutors from Vajiram & Ravi.

11 Christopher McFadden. 2023. 'From DVDs to Streaming, Here's the Incredible History of Netflix'. Interesting Engineering, 1 March. Available at: https://interestingengineering.com/culture/the-fascinating-history-of-netflix (accessed on 1 January 2024).

12 Raustiala and Sprigman. 2019. 'The Second Digital Disruption'.

13 Raustiala and Sprigman. 2019. 'The Second Digital Disruption'.

14 This is from personal experience and interviews with riders and drivers. However, this is available in public sources too. Also see Anirban Sen. 2017. 'Ola Losses Tripled to Rs 2,313 Crore during 2015-16 on Discounts, Driver Incentives', Livemint. 1 May. Available at: https://www.livemint.com/Companies/JNZ62LTm96hTej2STtAprK/Ola-losses-tripled-to-Rs-2313-during-201516-Tofler-report.html

15 Taxmann. 2022. 'Discounts Offered by Flipkart.com to Buyers Aren't Intangible Assets: ITAT'. In '25 Best Income-Tax Judgements in the Year 2018'. Available at: https://www.taxmann.com/post/blog/739/25-best-income-tax-judgements-in-the-year-2018 (accessed on 7 December 2023).

16 Taxmann. 2022. 'Discounts Offered by Flipkart.com to Buyers Aren't Intangible Assets'.

17 Jean-Charles Rochet and Jean Tirole. 2004. 'Two-Sided Markets: An Overview'. Available at: https://web.mit.edu/14.271/www/rochet_tirole.pdf (accessed on 16 August 2021).

18 Tanishka Sodhi. 2021. '"We Are Slaves to Them": Zomato, Swiggy Delivery Workers Speak Up against Unfair Practices'. Newslaundry, 14 August. Available at: https://www.newslaundry.com/2021/08/14/we-are-slaves-to-them-zomato-swiggy-delivery-workers-speak-up-against-unfair-practices (accessed on 16 August 2021).

19 Naomi Canton. 2021. 'Uber Drivers in UK to Get "Worker" Benefits'. *Times of India*, 18 March. Available at: https://timesofindia.indiatimes.com/business/international-business/uber-drivers-in-uk-to-get-pension-holiday-pay-and-be-guaranteed-rs-878-hourly-minimum-wage/articleshow/81556911.cms#:~:text=LONDON%3A%20Uber%20drivers%20in%20Britain,wage%20when%20driving%20with%20Uber (accessed on 29 August 2021).

20 The NFX Team. 2021. 'The Network Effects Manual: 16 Network Effects (And Counting)'. Available at: https://www.nfx.com/post/network-effects-manual/ accessed on 30 August 2023.

21 Antonio Madureira, Frank den Hartog, Harry Bouwman and Nico Baken. 2013. 'Empirical Validation of Metcalfe's Law: How Internet Usage Patterns Have Changed over Time'. *Information Economics and Policy*, 25 (4): 246–256.

22 Bismah Malik. 2020. 'Local Rivals Eat into Market Share of TikTok'. *New Indian Express*, 9 December. Available at: https://www.newindianexpress.com/business/2020/dec/09/local-rivals-eat-into-market-share-of-tiktok-2233732.html (accessed on 30 August 2021).

23 Bismah Malik. 2020. 'Local Rivals'.

24 Mohit Rana. 2021. 'The Rise of Made in India Digital Content'. Redseer, 21 April. Available at: https://redseer.com/reports/the-rise-of-made-in-india-digital-content/ (accessed on 30 August 2021).

25 Alex Moazed and Nicholas L. Johnson. 2017. *Modern Monopolies: What It Takes to Dominate the 21st Century Economy*. US: Macmillan.

26 OECD. 2018. 'Tax and Digitalisation'. Policy note available at: https://www.oecd.org/tax/beps/tax-and-digitalisation-policy-note.pdf (accessed on 1 September 2021). This note describes large digital business models as 'scale without mass'. In the context of taxation, it argues that these highly digital businesses can deeply engage in economic activities in a jurisdiction without having any 'mass' or physical presence in the jurisdiction. Although this phrase is frequently used in tax literature, it is generally not used in business literature.

27 G. Seetharaman. 2021. 'For Better or Worse: The Tata-BigBasket Marriage of Convenience'. The Ken. Available at: https://the-ken.com/story/for-better-or-worse-the-tata-bigbasket-marriage-of-convenience/ (accessed on 1 September 2021).

28 Of course, it is not fair to judge strengths and weaknesses of BigBasket's strategy purely based on its losses. The company has expanded significantly in its decade of operations and has been incurring significant capital expenses on developing new supply chains in new markets. Its fundamentals can be judged

better from its EBITDA earnings and segment results in markets where it is operational for a long time.

29 G. Seetharama. 2021. 'Dmart's E-commerce Tortoise Squares Off against the Jiomart Hare'. The Ken, 16 August. Available at: https://the-ken.com/story/dmarts-e-commerce-tortoise-squares-off-against-the-jiomart-hare/?searchTerm=Dmart (accessed on 1 September 2021).

30 G. Seetharama and Pranav Balakrishnan. 2021. 'A Year After Its Launch, Jiomart's E-commerce Book Is Still in Its First Chapter. The Ken, 21 May. Available at: https://the-ken.com/story/a-year-after-its-launch-jiomarts-e-commerce-book-is-still-in-its-first-chapter/?searchTerm=jiomart (accessed on 1 September 2021).

31 Jaclyn Robinson. '7 Failed Start Ups and the Lessons Learned'. Available at: https://about.crunchbase.com/blog/failed-startups-and-lessons-learned/ (accessed on 19 September 2021).

32 Gargi Sarkar. 2023. 'JioMart Customers Surge 9X Since Launch on WhatsApp in 2022: Isha Ambani'. Inc42, 28 August. Available at: https://inc42.com/buzz/jiomart-customers-surge-9x-since-launch-on-whatsapp-in-2022-isha-ambani/ (accessed on 1 January 2024).

33 Gargi Sarkar. 2023. 'JioMart Customers Surge'.

34 Ken Cottrill. 2006. 'When the Market Is Fragmented, Jump on a Platform'. *Harvard Business Publishing Newsletters*, 1 February. Available at: https://hbsp.harvard.edu/product/P0602C-PDF-ENG (accessed on 4 January 2024).

35 Geoffrey Parker and Marshall Van Alstyne. n.d. 'The Rise of Platform Economics: A Seismic Shift in Business Models'. Platform Revolution. Available at: https://platformthinkinglabs.com/materials/platform-economics/ (accessed on 19 September 2021).

Chapter 3 Platform Power

1 Kanoon. 'Rubtub Solutions Pvt. Ltd vs Makemytrip India Pvt. Ltd. (Mmt) & ... on 24 February, 2020'. Available at: https://indiankanoon.org/doc/111766104/ (accessed on 12 December 2023).

2 Kanoon. 'Rubtub Solutions'. Para 9.

3 Kanoon. 'Rubtub Solutions'.
4 Kanoon. 'Rubtub Solutions'.
5 Kanoon. 'Rubtub Solutions'.
6 Kanoon. 'Rubtub Solutions'. Para 15.
7 Kanoon. 'Rubtub Solutions'.
8 Statista Research Department. 2023. 'Value of Merger and Acquisitions (M&A) Deals Valued over One Billion U.S. Dollars Worldwide from 1985 to 2020'. *Statista*, 8 December. Available at: https://www.statista.com/statistics/966677/ (accessed on 11 December 2023).
9 Soha Goyal. 2021. 'Disney v. The Public Domain: How Mickey Mouse Keeps Changing Its Copyrights'. ipleaders, 18 July. Available at: https://blog.ipleaders.in/disney-v-public-domain-mickey-mouse-keeps-changing-copyrights/ (accessed on 12 December 2023).
10 Jonathan Tepper and Denise Hearn. 2019. *The Myth of Capitalism: Monopolies and the Death of Competition*. Hoboken, New Jersey: Wiley.
11 Ram Shivakumar. 2017. 'The Market Power of "Superstar" Companies Is Growing', *Chicago Booth Review*, 26 October. Available at: https://review.chicagobooth.edu/economics/2017/article/market-power-superstar-companies-growing (accessed on 11 December 2023).
12 Adrian Wooldridge. 2016. 'The Rise of Superstars'. *The Economist*, 15 September. Available at: https://www.economist.com/special-report/2016/09/15/the-rise-of-the-superstars (accessed on 11 December 2023).
13 Mukhisa Kituyi. 2018. 'Trade and Development Report 2018'. UNCTAD. Available at: https://unctad.org/webflyer/trade-and-development-report-2018 (accessed on 11 December 2023).
14 K. Pushpangadan and N. Shanta. 2009. *The Dynamics of Competition: Understanding India's Manufacturing Sector*. New Delhi: Oxford University Press; Suma Athreye and Sandeep Kapur. 2006. 'Industrial Concentration in a Liberalising Economy: A Study of Indian Manufacturing'. *Journal of Development Studies*, 42(6): 981–99.
15 Beena Saraswathy. 2019. 'Economic Reforms and Market Competition in India: An Assessment'. *Institute for Studies in Industrial Development*, December. Available at: https://isid.

org.in/wp-content/uploads/2020/04/WP216.pdf (accessed on 20 October 2021).

16 Smarak Swain and Suranjali Tandon. 2020. 'Applying the Turnover Filter in Transfer Pricing'. International Transfer Pricing Journal 27 (5). https://www.ibfd.org/shop/journal/applying-turnover-filter-transfer-pricing (accessed on 5 January 2024).

17 Ramesh Jangili. 2020.' Profitability in Emerging Markets: Efficiency or Market Power? A Study of Indian Firms'. Indira Gandhi Institute of Development Research, January. Available at: http://www.igidr.ac.in/pdf/publication/WP-2020-003.pdf (accessed on 19 October 2021).

18 Feng Zhu and Marco Iansiti. 2019. 'Why Some Platforms Thrive and Others Don't'. *Harvard Business Review*, January–February, 118–125. Available at: https://hbr.org/2019/01/why-some-platforms-thrive-and-others-dont (accessed on 11 December 2023).

19 Express News Service. '18 Months after Acquisition, Ola Shuts TaxiForSure; 700 Likely to Get Pink Slips'. *Indian Express*, 18 August, Available at: https://indianexpress.com/article/business/companies/18-months-after-acquisition-ola-shuts-taxiforsure-700-likely-to-get-pink-slips/ (accessed on 5 January, 2022).

20 Zhu & Iansiti. 2019. 'Why Some Platforms Thrive'.

21 Competition Commission of India. 2022. 'Case No. 39 of 2018'. Available at: https://www.cci.gov.in/antitrust/orders/details/1070/0 (accessed on 11 December 2023).

22 Reuters. 2021. 'Google Abused Android Dominance, Competition Commission of India Report Finds'. *The Hindu*, 18 September. Available at: https://www.thehindu.com/sci-tech/technology/google-abused-android-dominance-competition-commission-of-india-report-finds/article36535148.ece (accessed on 7 January 2022).

23 Competition Commission of India 2022. 'CCI imposes a Monetary Penalty of Rs. 936.44 Crore on Google for Anti-Competitive Practices in Relation to Its Play Store Policies'. *Press Information Bureau*, 25 October. Available at: https://pib.gov.in/PressReleasePage.aspx?PRID=1870819 (accessed on 21 January 2023).

24 *The Economist*. 2022. 'A Good Idea, Until It Isn't', 15–21 January.

Chapter 4 Platform Vulnerabilities

1 Ravindra Sonavane. 2021. 'Morgan Stanley Initiates Overweight Rating on Paytm; Sets Target Price at Rs. 1875'. Moneycontrol, 22 December. Available at: https://www.moneycontrol.com/news/business/markets/morgan-stanley-initiates-overweight-rating-on-paytm-sets-target-price-at-rs-1875-7852891.html (accessed on 25 January 2022).

2 Ravindra Sonavane. 2022. 'Morgan Stanley Reduces Stake in Paytm Substantially'. Moneycontrol, 21 January. Available at: https://www.moneycontrol.com/news/business/ipo/morgan-stanley-reduces-stake-in-paytm-substantially-7969001.html (accessed on 25 January 2022).

3 Swaminathan S. Anklesaria Aiyar. 2022. 'SwamiSpeak: In a Market So Full of Madness, a Big Global Stock Market Crash Is Coming'. *Economic Times*, 26 January. Available at: https://economictimes.indiatimes.com/opinion/et-commentary/view-a-big-global-stock-market-crash-is-coming/articleshow/89123853.cms?from=mdr (accessed on 27 January 2022).

4 Kanoon. 'Y.S. Jagan Mohan Reddy vs C.B.I. on 9 May 2013'. Available accessed on 15.02.2022 at: https://indiankanoon.org/doc/183369852/ (accessed on 15 February 2022).

5 *Business Standard*. 'What Is ONDC'. Available at: https://www.business-standard.com/about/what-is-ondc (accessed on 12 December 2023).

6 Reuters. 2021. 'Visa Complains to US Govt about India Backing for Local Rival RuPay'. *Times of India*, 28 November. Available at: https://timesofindia.indiatimes.com/business/india-business/visa-complains-to-us-govt-about-india-backing-for-local-rival-rupay/articleshow/87959679.cms (accessed on 12 December 2023).

7 A. Suri. 2022. *Great Tech Game: Shaping Geopolitics and the Destinies of Nations*. Gurgaon: HarperCollins.

8 Alex Capri. 2020. 'Strategic US-China Decoupling in the Tech Sector: Why and How It Is Happening'. Henrich Foundation. Available at: 'https://www.andrewleunginternationalconsultants.com/files/hinrich-foundation-strategic-technology-decoupling-from-china-alex-capri-08-june2020.pdf (accessed on 12 December 2023).

9 Le Rong. 2018. 'China: Doing Business in China: Technology Transfer Via Licensing Involving Chinese Parties'. Mondaq 9 August. Available at: https://www.mondaq.com/china/patent/725374/doing-business-in-china-technology-transfer-via-licensing-involving-chinese-parties (accessed on 12 December 2023).

10 A. Suri. 2022. *Great Tech Game*. Suri alludes to a military–civil fusion in China, the practice of the Chinese State to compel private companies to support its intelligence initiatives.

11 Many Indian start-ups are headquartered abroad due to business, tax and regulatory reasons; Anuj Suvarna and Joseph Rai. 2022. 'Almost 20% of India's "100 Unicorns" Headquartered Overseas, Few No Longer Unicorns'. VCCircle, 3 May. Available at: https://www.vccircle.com/almost-20-of-india-s-100-unicorns-headquartered-overseas-few-no-longer-unicorns (accessed on 13 December 2023).

12 K.W. Kapp. 1963. *Hindu Culture, Economic Development and Social Planning in India*. New York: Asia.

13 Ha-Joon Chang. 2011. *23 Things*.

Chapter 5 Crypto Evangelism

1 David Voreacos. 2022. 'BitConnect Promoter Gets 38 Months in $2.4 Billion Ponzi Scam'. Bloomberg, 17 September. Available at: https://www.bloomberg.com/news/articles/2022-09-17/bitconnect-promoter-gets-38-months-in-2-4-billion-ponzi-scam (accessed on 13 December 2023).

2 Mahesh Langa. 2018. 'The Bitcoin Probe Unravelling in Surat Is a Pandora's Box'. *The Hindu*, 26 May. Available at: https://www.thehindu.com/news/national/other-states/the-bitcoin-probe-unravelling-in-surat-is-a-pandoras-box/article61832195.ece (accessed on 13 December 2023).

3 Outlook Web Bureau. 2018. 'Mastermind in Gujarat Bitcoin Case Arrested'. *Outlook*, 4 May. Available at: https://www.outlookindia.com/website/story/mastermind-in-gujarat-bitcoin-case-arrested/311661 (accessed on 13 December 2023).

4 'Case 1:21-cv-07349, Document 1, Filed 09/01/21'. Available at: https://www.sec.gov/litigation/complaints/2021/comp-pr2021-172.pdf (accessed on 7 October 2022).

5 'Case 1:21-cv-07349, Document 1, Filed 09/01/21'.

6 Carl Brooker, Lisa Sanniti and Mark Pletcher. 2022. 'U.S. Promoter of Foreign Cryptocurrency Company Sentenced to Prison for Role in Fraud Scheme'. United States Attorney Office, 16 September. Available at: https://www.justice.gov/usao-sdca/pr/us-promoter-foreign-cryptocurrency-company-sentenced-prison-role-fraud-scheme (accessed on 7 October 2022).

7 'Case 1:21-cv-07349, Document 1, Filed 09/01/21'. Page 17.

8 Thomas Orlik. 2020. *China: The Bubble That Never Pops*. 156. New York: Oxford University Press.

9 Please note that this is not a recommendation to invest in cryptocurrencies.

10 The identity of the person or group of persons who goes by the name of 'Satoshi Nakamoto' is not known. It may be a single person, male or female, or a group of persons who founded bitcoin.

11 Jeff John Roberts. 2020. *Kings of Crypto: One Startup's Quest to Take Cryptocurrency out of Silicon Valley and onto Wall Street*. Boston, Massachusetts: Harvard Business Review Press.

12 Jeff John Roberts. 2020. *Kings of Crypto*.

13 Saylor.org. n.d. 'With Bit Gold, Szabo Was Inches Away from Inventing Bitcoin'. Available at: https://learn.saylor.org/mod/book/view.php?id=30735&chapterid=6704 (accessed on 14 December 2023).

14 A proof-of-work protocol is a blockchain consensus mechanism in which miners are incentivised for contributing computational power to validate transactions; Ameer Rosic. 2023. 'Proof of Work vs Proof of Stake: Basic Mining Guide', 23 November. Available at: https://blockgeeks.com/guides/proof-of-work-vs-proof-of-stake/ (accessed on 9 January 2024).

15 Nakamoto acknowledged this on the Bitcointalk forum in 2010; Saylor.org. n.d. 'With Bit Gold'.

16 Satoshi Nakamoto. 2008. 'Bitcoin: A Peer-to-Peer Electronic Cash System'. Available at: https://bitcoin.org/bitcoin.pdf (accessed on 29 October 2022).

17 Satoshi Nakamoto. 2008. 'Bitcoin'.

18 David Adler. 2018. 'Silk Road: The Dark Side of Cryptocurrency'. *Fordham Journal of Corporate and Financial Law*, 21 February. Available at: https://news.law.fordham.edu/jcfl/2018/02/21/

silk-road-the-dark-side-of-cryptocurrency/ (accessed on 30 October 2022).

19 Marwa Alnasaa, Nikolay Gueorguiev, Jiro Honda, Eslem Imamoglu, Paolo Mauro, Keyra Primus and Dmitriy L. Rozhkov. 2022. 'Crypto, Corruption, and Capital Controls: CrossCountry Correlations'. IMF Working Papers. Working Paper No. 2022/060. Available at: https://www.imf.org/en/Publications/WP/Issues/2022/03/25/Crypto-Corruption-and-Capital-Controls-Cross-Country-Correlations-515676 (accessed on 30 October 2022).

20 Press Trust of India. 2022. *Business Standard*, 30 October. Available at: https://www.business-standard.com/article/current-affairs/odisha-govt-officer-held-for-possessing-crypto-worth-over-rs-1-75-crore-122103000013_1.html (accessed on 30 October 2022).

21 Cassian Baliarsingh. 2022. 'Rs 8 cr Properties & Rs 1.75 cr Cryptocurrencies: Odisha Engineer's House a Corruption Den'. odishatv.in, 29 October. Available at: https://odishatv.in/news/miscellaneous/rs-8cr-properties-rs-1-75cr-cryptocurrencies-odisha-engineer-s-house-a-corruption-den-189021 (accessed on 30 October 2022).

22 The value of a virtual asset with a limited quantity in circulation may be pumped up artificially before the manipulators ultimately encash their holdings, leading to a drop in its market value (in a typical pump-and-dump fraud). This risk is inherent in decentralised virtual assets and manifests as high volatility in the prices of such assets.

23 U.S. Supreme Court. 1946. 'SEC v. W.J. Howey Co., 328 U.S. 293 (1946)'. Justia. Available at: https://supreme.justia.com/cases/federal/us/328/293/ (accessed on 15 December 2023).

24 American Bar Association. 2020. 'Digital and Digitized Assets: Federal and State Jurisdictional Issues, Derivatives and Futures Law Committee, Innovative Digital Products and Processes Subcommittee Jurisdiction Working Group'. 116.

25 A fiat currency is a national currency backed by promise of the country's government to honour its value.

26 Ric Edelman. 2022. *The Truth about Crypto: Your Investing Guide to Understanding Blockchain, Bitcoin, and Other Digital Assets*. New York: Simon & Schuster.

27 Ric Edelman. 2022. *The Truth about Crypto.*

28 Ric Edelman. 2022. *The Truth about Crypto.*

29 FATF. 2020. 'FATF Report to the G20 Finance Ministers and Central Bank Governors on So-Called Stablecoins'. Available at: https://www.fatf-gafi.org/media/fatf/documents/recommendations/Virtual-Assets-FATF-Report-G20-So-Called-Stablecoins.pdf (accessed on 4 November 2022).

Chapter 6 Crypto Elitism

1 Varghese Jacob, Sailendra Prasanna Mishra and Suresh Radhakrishnan. 2019. 'Is Decentralization Sustainable in the Bitcoin System?' SSRN, 30 October. Available at: http://dx.doi.org/10.2139/ssrn.3478373 (accessed on 15 December 2023).

2 Lukka. n.d. 'Robust Data Management for the Digital Asset'. Available at: https://lukka.tech/enterprise-software/ (accessed on 15 December 2023).

3 FATF does not actually impose sanctions on grey-listed or black-listed countries. It requires its members and other countries in its global network to do enhanced due diligence of transactions in their respective jurisdictions with grey-listed and black-listed countries. As a result, such transactions are marked risky and are subject to intense scrutiny by financial institutions. This leads to many adverse consequences for the financial system of grey-listed and black-listed countries.

4 FATF. 2020. 'FATF Report'.

5 FATF. 2020. 'FATF Report'.

6 Don Tapscott and Alex Tapscott. 2016. *Blockchain Revolution: How the Technology Behind Bitcoin Is Changing Money, Business and the World*. New York: Portfolio Penguin.

7 Pawan Nahar. 2022. FTX Failure Wipes Out over $150 Billion from Crypto M-cap; Gloomy Road for the Rattled Investors'. *The Economic Times*, 9 November. Available at: https://economictimes.indiatimes.com/markets/cryptocurrency/ftx-failure-wipes-out-over-150-billion-from-crypto-m-cap-gloomy-road-for-the-rattled-investors/articleshow/95406032.cms?from=mdr (accessed on 3 January 2023).

8 Anthony Clarke. 2022. '7 Biggest Crypto Collapses of 2022 the Industry Would Like to Forget'. Cointelegraph, 26 December. Available at: https://cointelegraph.com/

news/7-biggest-crypto-collapses-of-2022-the-industry-would-like-to-forget (accessed on 3 January 2023).

9 These facts were found after the exchange went bust, when debtors took control of the exchange and conducted their own due diligence. The debtors' first report, titled 'First Interim Report of John J. Ray III to the Independent Directors on Control Failures at the FTX Exchanges' was released on 9 April 2023. Available at: https://storage.courtlistener.com/recap/gov.uscourts.deb.188450/gov.uscourts.deb.188450.1242.1.pdf (accessed on 15 May 2023).

10 Market makers traded in cryptocurrencies to satisfy market demand.

11 Oladeinde Olawoyin. 2022. 'Nigeria, Indonesia, Five Others Home to Half of World's Unbanked Population', *Premium Times*, 25 August. Available at: https://www.premiumtimesng.com/business/business-news/550585-nigeria-indonesia-five-others-home-to-half-of-worlds-unbanked-population.html (accessed on 7 January 2023).

12 Aprajita Verma. 2021. 'RBI Report: India's 'Financial Inclusion Index' Is 53.9 by the end of March 2021'. Factly, 28 August. Available at: https://factly.in/rbi-report-indias-financial-inclusion-index-is-53-9-by-the-end-of-march-2021/ (accessed on 7 January 2023).

13 Rhian Lewis. 2020. *The Crypto-Currency Revolution: Finance in the Age of Bitcoin, Blockchains and Tokens*. London: Kogan Page; Lewis says, 'Lack of common standards is the biggest barrier to seamless international payments. SWIFT is not convinced that blockchain technology will solve this problem, so their efforts towards instantaneous real-time payments, 24/7, are focused on more mundane initiatives such as adopting the ISO 20022 standard, using OpenAPIs and standardising technical architecture across borders and institutions.'

14 Privacy coins have been delisted from exchanges in many countries because of their anonymity-enhancing features; Prashant Jha. 2022. 'Regulations and Exchange Delistings Put Future of Private Cryptocurrencies in Doubt'. Cointelegraph, 16 June. Available at: https://cointelegraph.com/news/regulations-and-exchange-delistings-put-future-of-private-cryptocurrencies-in-doubt (accessed on 15 January 2023).

15 Talking about the way Vitalik Butelin's idea for the Ethereum platform evolved, Matthey Leising says, 'Vitalik knew that there would be people who would want to try to overwhelm Ethereum, to slow it down or even break it entirely, by spamming it with thousands of simultaneous transactions. If they wanted to do that, they'd have to pay a hefty fee in the form of ether. Gas was the main idea here, like what you put in your car. No gas, no go.'; Matthew Leising. 2021. *Out of the Ether: The Amazing Story of Ethereum and the $55 Million Heist That Almost Destroyed It All.* New Jersey: Wiley.

16 Stuart D. Levi and Alex B. Lipton. 2018. 'An Introduction to Smart Contracts and Their Potential and Inherent Limitations'. Harvard Law School Forum on Corporate Governance. Available at: https://corpgov.law.harvard.edu/2018/05/26/an-introduction-to-smart-contracts-and-their-potential-and-inherent-limitations/ (accessed on 16 January 2023).

17 Greg Cipolaro and Ross Stevens. 2020. 'The Power of Bitcoin's NetworkEffects'.*NYDIGReport*,November.Availableat:https://assets-global.website-files.com/614e11536f66309636c98688/616c92ea37a2ff12923190c8_NYDIG-Power-of-Bitcoins-Network-Effect.pdf (accessed on 20 January 2023).

18 Greg Cipolaro and Ross Stevens. 2020. 'The Power of Bitcoin's Network Effects'.

19 Neil Hildreth. 2021. 'India: Cryptocurrency Bill 2021: The Road Ahead'. mondaq, 28 December. Available at: https://www.mondaq.com/india/fin-tech/1145012/cryptocurrency-bill-2021-the-road-ahead (accessed on 15 May 2023).

20 Neil Hildreth. 2021. 'India: Cryptocurrency Bill 2021'.

Chapter 7 Think Networks

1 Smarak Swain. 2019. *Loophole Games: A Treatise on Tax Avoidance Strategies* New Delhi: WoltersKluwer India.

2 The US Trade Representative (USTR) initiated Section 301 action against countries which imposed Digital Service Tax or Equalisation Levy. A press release by the Government of India on 7 January 2021 stated, 'India based e-commerce operators are already subject to taxes in India for revenue generated from the Indian market. However, in the absence of the EL, non-resident e-commerce operators (not having any Permanent

Establishment in India but significant economic presence) are not required to pay taxes in respect of the consideration received in the e-commerce supply or services made in the Indian market. The EL levied at 2% is applicable on non-resident e-commerce operator, not having a permanent establishment in India. The threshold for this levy is Rs. 2 crore, which is very moderate and applies equally to all e-commerce operators across the globe having business in India. The levy does not discriminate against any U.S. companies, as it applies equally to all non-resident e-commerce operators, irrespective of their country of residence. … The purpose of the Equalization Levy is to ensure fair competition, reasonableness and exercise the ability of governments to tax businesses that have a close nexus with the Indian market through their digital operations.' The press release is available at: https://pib.gov.in/Pressreleaseshare.aspx?PRID=1686865 (accessed on 12 January 2023).

3 OECD. 2019. 'Programme of Work to Develop a Consensus Solution to the Tax Challenges Arising from the Digitalisation of the Economy'. OECD Publishing, Paris, 31 May. Available at: https://www.oecd.org/tax/beps/programme-of-work-to-develop-a-consensus-solution-to-the-tax-challenges-arising-from-the-digitalisation-of-the-economy.htm (accessed on 12 January 2023).

4 OECD. 2020. 'Tax Challenges Arising from Digitalisation – Report on Pillar One Blueprint: Inclusive Framework on BEPS, OECD/G20 Base Erosion and Profit Shifting Project'. OECD Publishing, Paris. Available at: https://doi.org/10.1787/beba0634-en (accessed on 12.01.2023).

5 UN. 2020. 'Committee of Experts on International Cooperation in Tax Matters Twentieth session 20–23 and 26–29 October 2020'. Available at: https://www.superperfect.com/events/20th-session-committee-experts-international-cooperation-tax-matters (accessed on 9 January 2024); please refer to item 3(i) of the provisional agenda: 'Tax consequences of the digitalized economy – issues of relevance for developing countries'

6 This proposal had many other problems. For example, it was quite theoretical. It was introduced in the form of a new Article 12B in the UN Model Tax Treaty. To implement it, a country had to re-negotiate of its bilateral tax treaties.

7 OECD. 2022. 'Progress Report on Amount A of Pillar One: Two-Pillar Solution to the Tax Challenges of the Digitalisation of the Economy, OECD/G20 Base Erosion and Profit Shifting Project, OECD, Paris'. Available at: https://www.oecd.org/tax/beps/progress-report-on-amount-a-of-pillar-one-july-2022.pdf; OECD's progress report shows that the new regime was proposed to be applied not just for Automated Digital Services and Consumer Facing Businesses, but for the entire economy. To work, it requires businesses with turnover above US$20 billion to trace the sale of each good and service to a country of consumption.

8 Anna Isaac. 2022. 'UN Agrees Global Tax Rules Resolution Giving Developing Nations Greater Say'. *The Guardian*, 23 November. Available at: https://www.theguardian.com/world/2022/nov/23/un-agrees-global-tax-rules-resolution-giving-developing-nations-greater-say (accessed on 13 January 2023).

9 See, for example, the blueprint in OECD (2020). The blueprint says: 'Certain MNEs can generate revenue from the provision of [Automated Digital Services] (including revenue from the monetisation of data) that are provided on an automated and standardised basis to a large and global customer or user base and can do so remotely to customers in markets with little or no local infrastructure. They often exploit powerful customer or user network effects and generate substantial value from interaction with users and customers. They often benefit from data and content contributions made by users and from the intensive monitoring of users' activities and the exploitation of corresponding data.'

10 FATF says that peer-to-peer transactions represent 'residual risk'. This has been discussed in Chapter 5 in greater detail.

Epilogue

1 Vala Afshar. 2022. 'ARK Invest's Big Ideas 2022: The 14 Transformative Technologies to Watch This Year. ZDNET, 26 January. Available at: https://www.zdnet.com/article/ark-invest-big-ideas-2022/ (accessed on 1 January 2024).

Index

About the Author

A graduate of electrical engineering from IIT Kharagpur, Smarak Swain is an officer of the 2008 batch of the Indian Revenue Service who has served in various capacities in New Delhi, Bangalore and Bhubaneswar. He was part of India's negotiating team in OECD's Task Force on Digital Economy. In his current position, he supervises anti-money-laundering and counter-terrorist financing policies of India and also handles India's engagements with the Financial Action Task Force. He is involved in risk assessment of new and emerging technologies, regulatory gap analysis and design of regulation for new products.